PORTUGAL

Julia Wilkinson

Photography by Steve Vidler

Hong Kong

Grateful acknowledgement is made to the following authors and publishers for permissions granted:

Peter Owen Ltd for
A Visit to Portugal 1866 by Hans Christian Andersen, English translation © 1972 by Peter Owen Ltd and Grace Thornton
and
Travels in My Homeland by Almeida Garrett, translated by John M Parker, English translation © 1987 by UNESCO

Random Century Group for
When the Wolves Howl by Aquilino Ribeiro, translated by Patricia McGowan Pinheiro, English version © 1963 by Jonathan Cape Ltd

Atheneum Publishers, an imprint of Macmillan Publishing Company for
Salazar Blinks © 1988 by David Slavitt

Distribution in the United Kingdom, Ireland, Europe and certain Commonwealth countries by Hodder and Stoughton, Mill Road, Dunton Green, Sevenoaks, Kent TN13 2YA

British library Cataloguing in Publication Data has been applied for.

Editor: May Holdsworth
Series Editor: Claire Banham
Illustrations Editor: Caroline Robertson
Map Artwork: Bai Yiliang
Design: U Wang Graphics
Cover Concept: Raquel Jaramillo and Aubrey Tse
Additional Photography courtesy of Centro de Arte Moderna, Lisbon: 161, 188; Calouste Gulbenkian Museum, Lisbon: 72; sketches courtesy of Caroline Jones: 47, 134-135; Museu de Marinha, Lisbon: 51. 85 (top right), 180; Sebastião Salgado/Magnum Photos, Paris: 10-11, 91; The Board of Trustees of the Victoria and Albert Museum, London: 149; Julia Wilkinson: 80 (top right), 88 (below), 98 (right), 107, 113, 138, 198

Production House: Twin Age Limited, Hong Kong
Printed in Hong Kong by Sing Cheong Printing Co., Ltd.

PORTUGAL

Acknowledgments

My thanks must first go to the Portuguese National Tourist Office and especially to Mrs Pilar Pereira in the London office, and the staff in the local offices of Coimbra, Évora, Oporto, Bragança, and Vila do Conde. In Oporto, Mr João de Freitas and his team from the Institute of Promotion for Tourism provided enormous assistance—and with such passionate enthusiasm for their northern region that I was left in doubt that this was indeed somewhere special. Finally, my gratitude goes to John at home for his support and scrupulous editing and to all those whom I met on the road and who shared with me their discoveries and knowledge.

Contents

Western Europe

The legendary cockrel of Barcelos (above); an azulejo *panel celebrating the monastic skill of wine-making (below); girls dress for a festival in Chamula (right)*

Excerpts

Portugal
(Province Map)

N

0 25 50 75 km

0 25 50 miles

MINHO

Viana do Castelo

Bragança

Minho

Lima

Cávado

Tâmega

Braga

TRÁS-OS-MONTES

Vila Real

Porto

DOURO

Douro

Tua

Sabor

Vouga

BEIRA ALTO

Côa

Ria de Aveiro

Viseu

Aveiro

Guarda

mondego

Coimbra

BEIRA LITORAL

BEIRA BAIXA

SPAIN

Zêzere

Leiria

Castelo Branca

Tagus

Atlantic Ocean

Tomar

RIBATEJO

Portalegre

ESTREMADURA

Sántarém

Sorraia

Sintra

Elvas

LISBON

SETUBAL

Évora

ALENTEJO

Sines

Guadiana

Beja

Sado

Odemira

Mira

Alcoutim

Sevilla

Portimão

ALGARVE

Albufeira

Lagos

Sagres

Faro

Gulf of Cádiz

© The Guidebook Company Ltd

Introduction

Perched at the end of the Iberian peninsula, in the westernmost corner of Europe, Portugal has always been a land apart, on the fringe, lining the forgotten hem of Europe. No insurmountable barriers separate it from Spain. Only a strip of water keeps Africa away. It might have been snapped up long ago, a tasty morsel for the Moors of Morocco or the Kings of Castile. It almost was. But Portugal is a plucky little place. It established its frontiers as long ago as the thirteenth century, which makes it one of the oldest countries in Europe. The very earliest historical evidence shows a determination to keep invaders at bay. And a later independent spirit was to turn this tiny country—not much bigger than Austria or the state of Indiana—away from Europe entirely and out into the unknown world, changing the course of history with its discovery of the sea route to India.

The fifteenth-century Age of Discoveries gave Portugal a mystique of power and glory that it never quite relinquished, despite the loss of most of its empire a century later and its near-escape from being swallowed up by Spain, and then France. But in more recent times, it escaped attention, too—always that little bit too far to be included in the European Grand Tour, or too often wracked by political turmoil.

Only slowly, since the late 1970s, has Portugal started to emerge from the shadows, to tug at the hem of Europe: in 1986 it became a member of the European Community and began, for the first time in 500 years, to look to a future within Europe.

Now, too, there is a growing realization among travellers that here is a country left untapped for decades, a country of extraordinary diversity, with high mountain peaks and plains of cork trees, rich green valleys and swathes of lushness, 'the garden of Europe,' wrote Coleridge, 'planted by the seashore.' To walk in this garden (and not just along the Algarvian seashore) is a remarkable experience: for here you can find traditions unchanged for centuries, a way of life still bound up with the land, the family, the church. Much is changing, of course, and changing fast. But nowhere else in Europe can you find a country with so many unspoilt corners, so strong an independent spirit.

This book aims to guide you on a twentieth-century journey of discovery, not only to Portugal's famous places but also 'Off the Track' to some of those hidden corners. With luck, you might get lost en route and discover a piece of unspoilt magic for yourself.

Background
History

From Romans to Revolution
The Lusitani and Life Under the Romans
On a strangely silent hilltop in the north of Portugal, not far from god-fearing Braga city, you can stand in the circles of Portugal's past: a stone-walled fortified village. Dozens of these *citânias* have been found in northern Portugal, often revealing huge defensive walls and several moats.

These first permanent settlements, dating back to around 800 BC, were inhabited by native tribes and Celts. Meanwhile, in the south, Phoenician traders, followed by Greeks and Carthaginians, set up coastal stations and mined metals inland until the Romans arrived in 210 BC and took control.

But not without a struggle. The Lusitani, a Celtic warrior tribe based between the Tagus and Douro rivers, gave the Romans a particularly hard time. Only after their leader Viriatus was assassinated in 139 BC did resistance collapse. The name 'Lusitania' lived on as one of the later Roman provinces, encompassing nearly all of present-day Portugal.

Julius Caesar made Olisipo (Lisbon) the capital in 60 BC; other major colonies were Ebora (Évora), Bracara Augusta (Braga) and Pax Julia (Beja). In the autumn of their rule, Christianity was also established, with important bishoprics at Évora and Braga.

Although only a few great Roman sites of interest remain—particularly the Temple of Diana at Évora, and the defensive settlement of Conimbriga near Coimbra—the legacy of 400 years of Roman rule shows in many of Portugal's roads and bridges, in the crops they introduced (wheat, barley and the vine) and above all in the language which is heavily derived from Latin.

With the decline of the Roman Empire in the early fifth century, a wave of barbarian invaders swept through Spain and Portugal from beyond the Pyrenees—the Vandals, Alans, Suevi and Visigoths.

The Suevi soon became the dominant force. But around AD 585 the Visigoths got the upper hand. For over a century they maintained a tenuous rule over most of the peninsula. Internal divisions finally led to an appeal for aid from the Moors of Africa who were only too ready to move northwards. Unlike the Visigoths, these Islamic forces were to have an overwhelming impact on Portugal and its culture.

The Moors and How Christianity Fought Back
The first Moors arrived in 711. They swept through Spain and into Europe, across the old abandoned Roman provinces. In Portugal, the Moors reached as far as Aveiro but mostly settled in the south, particularly the al-Gharb (Algarve)

coastal region, where they made Shelb (Silves) their capital. This was a civilizing and productive time for Portugal. The Moors (mostly Berbers, but also Egyptians and Syrians) were tolerant of both Jews and Christians. They introduced new crops (fruit and rice) and new methods of irrigation, and left a legacy of Arabic words and cuisine. But in the early eleventh century, Spain and northern Portugal became a battlefield for the rival faiths: the Christians edging in from the north, and fanatical Muslims from the south.

In fact, the Christians had begun the 'Reconquista' long before, with a small but symbolic victory in 718 at Covadonga in the northern mountainous area of Spain. Around this Christian base, the small kingdom of Asturias-Leon slowly expanded, eluding Muslim domination. It gradually took over Castile, Aragon, Galicia, and the land of 'Portucale' (between the Minho and the Douro). By the eleventh century Portucale had become a powerful county in its own right.

In 1085, Alfonso VI (emperor of all these Christian kingdoms) took the bull by the horns and conquered the Moors in their Spanish heartland at Toledo. A colourful character, Alfonso is said to have gambled on securing Seville by playing a game of chess with its cultured emir (he is also said to have married the emir's daughter). But the next year, Alfonso faced a tougher enemy: the ruthless Almoravids from Morocco who answered the emir's call for help.

The Almoravids defeated Alfonso, and installed a harsh government, driving out the Christian inhabitants, called Mozarabs, who had previously been tolerated. They were followed by the Almohads: an even more fanatical, reforming Berber sect who detested the Almoravids and were prepared for an all-out attack on Christian Spain.

Now it was Alfonso's turn to call on supporters: European crusaders rallied to fight the infidels. Among them were Henri of Burgundy and his cousin Raymond, who were rewarded for their efforts with land and marriage to Alfonso's daughters. Raymond was given Urraca and the lands of Galicia and Coimbra; Henri won Teresa and the territory of Portucale.

The liaisons led to a complicated war of succession. After Henri's death, Teresa favoured a union with Galicia, now ruled by Urraca's son, Alfonso VII. But her own son, Afonso Henriques, had more independent ideas. He defeated his mother's forces in 1128 near his capital at Guimarães, and set about consolidating his power by defeating the Moors in a series of battles. In 1143, Alfonso VII formally recognized him as the first King of Portugal, a title that was acknowledged by the Pope in 1179. Only Alentejo and the Algarve remained to be wrested from the Moors to complete the triumph.

Over the next century, Afonso's successors gradually brought victory to the Reconquista, helped by European crusaders and military-religious organizations like the Knights Templar. By 1249, western Algarve and Faro had fallen. In 1297, the boundaries of the kingdom (much the same as today) were officially recognized by the Spanish power, Castile. Portugal had come of age.

Dinis, King of the Castle

With the Moors out of the way, Portugal's Burgundian kings could concentrate
on social and political matters. They encouraged internal colonization in the
south (far less populated than the north), founded towns to guard the frontier
with Leon, and began to consult the clergy and nobility at assemblies or *cortes,*
the first being held in Coimbra (the then capital) in 1211.

But the greatest advances in Portugal's development undoubtedly came
during the reign of just one king: Dom Dinis (1279–1325). A far-sighted and
cultured man, Dinis shook Portugal into shape: he brought the judicial systems
under royal control, established a progressive programme of agricultural reform
and afforestation, reorganized the dangerously powerful Knights Templar into
the Order of Christ, and cultivated music, education and the arts.

Dinis also made it clear that Portugal was prepared to defend its new independence. He built 50 fortresses along the frontier with Castile, and signed a
pact of friendship with England in 1308 that was to be reconfirmed and called
on many times in the future to help secure Portugal's freedom.

It was none too soon. Within 60 years of Dinis' death, Portugal was at war
with Castile over rival claims to the Portuguese throne. Backed by the merchant
and peasant classes, João, a bastard heir of the Burgundian king Pedro I, fought
it out against the Castilians at the battle of Aljubarrota in 1385.

Even with the assistance of English archers, the odds were stacked against João's small army; he vowed to build a monastery to the Virgin if he won. The victory sealed Portugal's independence—and delivered the superb architectural legacy of Batalha Abbey. Relations with England were also cemented with the 1386 Treaty of Windsor followed by the marriage of João to Philippa of Lancaster, daughter of John of Gaunt. With hostile Castile to the east, Portugal was now forced to turn its back on the rest of the peninsula and look west: to seek its destiny in the Atlantic Ocean and the unknown world.

The Age of Discoveries

The first sign of a campaigning spirit came in 1415 with the capture of Ceuta in Morocco. A few years later, the Portuguese began to settle in Madeira, cultivating sugar and cereals (colonization of both Madeira and the Azores followed later in 1445). However, it was the activities of Prince Henry 'the Navigator' (a younger son of João) who gave Portugal the means to exploit this restlessness and change from a small kingdom to a great imperial power, one of the richest and most influential in the world.

'This is the story,' began Luís de Camões in his epic sixteenth-century poem, The Lusiads, 'of heroes who, leaving their native Portugal behind them, opened a way to Ceylon, and further, across seas no man had ever sailed before.' In fact, the reasons for Portugal's overseas expansion involve more than simple heroic adventurism. What spurred the first Portuguese explorers was rather a haphazard, vague combination of crusading zeal in the fight against infidels, profit-seeking for slaves and gold and spices, and love of martial glory.

At Prince Henry's school of navigation in Sagres, expeditions were organized and sent forth into the unknown. Shipbuilding, map-making, astronomy and navigation were developed and refined. In 1434, Gil Eanes sailed beyond the much-feared Cape Bojador on the west coast of Africa and discovered that the world did not fall into hell. The way was now open: by the 1460s the Cape Verde Islands were discovered and the Gulf of Guinea was reached. Finally, in 1487, Bartolomeu Dias rounded the Cape of Good Hope.

By this time, Castile had started to dispute some of Portugal's new conquests. In 1481, the Church ratified a treaty between them, eager to keep both sides at peace so that they could concentrate on reaching the African Christians, believed to exist under a mythical priest and king, Prester John.

But Columbus' discovery of America for Spain in 1492 set off a new round of disputes. The result was the extraordinary Treaty of Tordesillas of 1494 by which the world was divided between its two great powers, Spain and Portugal. The Pope gave his ruling: Spain was to have the unknown lands west of the line running 370 leagues west of the Cape Verde Islands. Portugal won the known world to the east—including Brazil, whose existence they may well have already secretly known about.

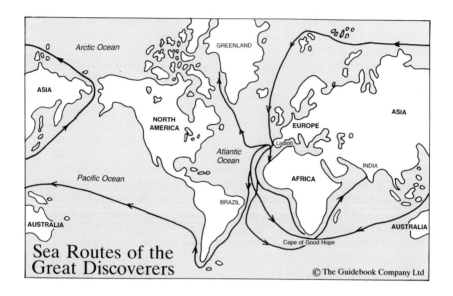

Sea Routes of the Great Discoverers

© The Guidebook Company Ltd

It was Portugal's moment of glory, the dawn of its Golden Age. No other time in history—not even the Cold War—has so blatantly established the spheres of influence in the world. And no other act has so set the stage for imperialism on a massive scale.

The Fabled East and the Empire's Fall

When young King Manuel came to the throne in 1495 he seized the spirit of the age and sent Vasco da Gama to find the sea route to India, a voyage which was to change the course of history. Cabral officially discovered Brazil in 1500, and by 1513 the Portuguese had reached Timor and China.

Under the brilliant strategist, Afonso de Albuquerque, Portugal built up its Asian empire with garrison ports and strategic trading posts: Goa was won in 1510; Malacca in 1511; Ormuz in 1515; and Macau in 1557. By then, Portugal dominated world trade. The monarchy, taking its 'royal fifth' of trading profits, became the richest in Europe, and a lavish 'Manueline' style of architecture marked the exuberance of the age, notably in the Jerónimos Monastery and Torre de Belém.

But the 1570s marked the beginning of the end. The riches went no further than the Crown and nobility, leaving little chance for an entrepreneurial class to develop. Domestic agriculture declined; prices in Europe fell, and the cost of the new empire soon left even the Crown in debt. The expulsion of many commercially-minded refugee Spanish Jews in 1496 and the later persecution of converted Jews ('New Christians') by the Inquisition helped the financial situation.

The final straw came when Dom Sebastiao took the throne in 1557 and foolishly set out on a new crusade against Morocco. In 1578 he was disastrously defeated, killed with over 8,000 others, including most of Portugal's nobility. What little was left in the coffers was spent over the next few years in ransoms for those captured.

Not surprisingly, Spain was waiting to pounce on the debilitated kingdom. In 1580, Sebastiao's uncle, Philip II of Spain, defeated a Portuguese force at the battle of Alcantara and the following year was crowned Felipe I of Portugal.

Independence Lost and Regained

Spain promised Portugal autonomy, and at first this was honoured. But Philip's successors were heavy-handed, raising men and money in Portugal for Spain's wars. Meanwhile, Portugal's empire was slipping away: the English won Ormuz in 1622, while the Dutch took Malacca in 1641 and Ceylon in the 1650s.

Discontent grew, leading to a coup in Lisbon in 1640 and a popular call for the reluctant but powerful Duke of Bragança to take the throne and end Spanish rule. As João IV, the duke succeeded in maintaining Portugal's fragile

independence (Spain was fortunately busy with wars elsewhere) and in renewing the alliance with Britain: by the Treaty of 1661, Charles II married Catherine of Bragança and Portugal ceded Tangier and Bombay. After various clashes, Spain finally recognized Portugal's independence again in 1668.

But overall it was a humiliating time for Portugal, with unrelenting economic depression, the continuing loss of empire and maritime trade, and increasing British control of profitable vineyards. The discovery of gold and diamonds in Brazil in the 1690s was the only bright spot, though once again the monarchy proceeded to spend most of the riches on lavish monuments, such as the vast baroque monastery palace of Mafra.

The time called for a ruthless ruler to save the economy. Under the hedonistic Dom José (who was more interested in opera than affairs of state), José's Chief Minister, the Marquês de Pombal took over. Pursuing a policy of enlightened despotism he steered Portugal towards a steadier economic course, boosting agriculture and industry, rebuilding Lisbon after the Great Earthquake of 1755, and abolishing slavery in the mainland. But any opposition was brutally put down.

Britain and Brazil: The New Masters

Pombal's dismissal by José's successor, the devout Maria I, put a stop to his religious reforms but his economic, agricultural and educational improvements were largely maintained. Increasingly, however, attention was directed to the turmoil of the French Revolution.

When Portugal sided with Britain and sent forces against France in 1793, Napoleon threatened to invade unless the Portuguese closed their ports to British shipping—an obviously impossible demand for Portugal since her trade (especially in cloth and wine) and shipping routes were now so dependent on her old ally. The Royal Family fled to Brazil, and the French invaded.

For the first time, the fight for Portugal's independence was led by foreigners: coming to the rescue, Britain's generals Wellesley (later Duke of Wellington) and Beresford commanded joint forces and finally forced the French back into Spain in 1811.

It was something of a Pyrrhic victory, as Portugal's weakened state allowed Brazil to be proclaimed a kingdom in 1815. Worse, in 1810 Portugal had been forced to allow Britain to trade directly with Brazil, thereby losing her profitable intermediary trading role. The Court remained in Brazil, and Beresford acted as Portugal's administrator. In effect, Portugal had become little more than a colony of Brazil and a protectorate of Britain.

Liberal Rebels and Warring Brothers

Ironically, it was Spain and France that helped revive Portugal's independent spirit. Inspired by those countries' liberal movements, a group of officers rebelled and in 1822 drew up a new Constitution, based on the ideals of the Enlightenment. On his return from Brazil, João VI accepted its terms. Trouble erupted after João's death in 1826. His son and heir, Pedro, Emperor of Brazil, abdicated in favour of his daughter, Maria, and drew up a new, less liberal Charter. He intended that Maria should marry her uncle, Miguel, who would rule as Regent under the new Constitution. Miguel, however, turned the tables on everyone: he abolished the Charter and proclaimed himself king. With the support of British, Spanish, French and Portuguese liberals, Pedro defeated Miguel in 1834 and took the throne, ending absolutism once and for all.

The Rocky Road to a Republic

The next 50 years, after Pedro's death in 1834, was a period of political turmoil. The victorious liberals divided into conservatives and progressives and squabbled over support for the 1822 Constitution or the 1826 Charter. Only English and Spanish intervention prevented civil war breaking out in 1846. Power was eventually shared between the two main parties.

Portugal tried to put itself in order, introducing industrialization and major public works programmes. But the African colonies (Cape Verde Islands, Guiné, São Tomé and Principe, Angola and Mozambique—all acquired during the Age of Discoveries)were still a tremendous drain, and economic development was slow. By 1890 the state was virtually bankrupt. Urban discontent grew; so too did support for socialism and trade unions. Republicanism among the urban lower-middle class became an increasing threat to the monarchist establishment.

After a failed Republican revolt in 1891, and the collapse of the power-sharing system, Dom Carlos ruled dictatorially but in 1908 the Republicans rose again and assassinated Carlos and his eldest son. Carlos' younger son Manuel tried to patch things up, but it was too late. The Republic thrust itself into existence and Manuel, 'the Unfortunate', sailed into exile in Britain.

The Republic and Rise of Salazar

'Oh sea heroes, oh noble people. . . raise again the splendour of Portugal. . !' The national anthem of 1910 revealed an idealistic optimism that was never fulfilled. Within 16 years there were 45 changes of government, installed by military intervention since neither the president nor prime minister had the power to dissolve parliament. The chaos ended any chance of economic stability.

Coups and counter-coups continued even during the First World War which Portugal entered on the Allied side. Finally, in 1926, the army took over and General Oscar Carmona was named President. But the man who had the real control was the finance minister, António de Oliveira Salazar. Having miraculously put the economy in order, he was made Prime Minister in 1932, a post he retained for 36 years.

Fire and Brimstone

After the earthquake which destroyed three-quarters of Lisbon, the wise men of that country could discover no more efficacious way of preventing a total ruin than by giving the people a splendid auto–da–fé. It was decided by the university of Coimbre that the sight of several persons being slowly burned in great ceremony is an infallible secret for preventing earthquakes. Consequently they had arrested a Biscayan convicted of having married his fellow-godmother, and two Portuguese who, when eating a chicken, had thrown away the bacon; after dinner they came and bound Dr. Pangloss and his disciple Candide, one because he had spoken and the other because he had listened with an air of approbation; they were both carried separately to extremely cool apartments, where there was never any discomfort from the sun; a week afterwards each was dressed in a sabenito and their heads were ornamented with paper mitres; Candide's mitre and sanbenito were painted with flames upside down and with devils who had neither tails nor claws; but Pangloss's devils had claws and tails, and his flames were upright. Dressed in this manner they marched in procession and listened to a most pathetic sermon, followed by lovely plain-song music. Candide was flogged in time to the music, while the singing went on; the Biscayan and the two men who had not wanted to eat bacon were burned, and Pangloss was hanged, although this is not the custom. The very same day, the earth shook again with a terrible clamour. Candide, terrified, dumbfounded, bewildered, covered with blood, quivering from head to foot, said to himself: "If this is the best of all possible worlds, what are the others? Let it pass that I was flogged, for I was flogged by the Bulgarians, but, O my dear Pangloss! The greatest of philosophers! The best of men! Was it necessary that you should be drowned in port! O Mademoiselle Cunegonde! The pearl of women! Was it necessary that your belly should be slit!" He was returning, scarcely able to support himself, preached at, flogged, absolved and blessed, when an old woman accosted him and said: "Courage, my son, follow me . . ."

Voltaire, Candide, *1929*

Salazar instituted a new Constitution, in effect a fascist regime: only one political association was permitted, censorship was strictly enforced, and opposition controlled by a secret police force. There were dozens of attempted coups by former Republicans but nothing that posed a serious threat to Salazar's firm grip on power.

In the Second World War, Portugal remained 'neutral', while granting the Allies strategic bases in the Azores and supplying wolfram to the Nazis—a policy that at least filled the coffers.

Opposition forces slowly gathered momentum, both internally and overseas. One long fuse ready to spark was Salazar's refusal to relinquish the colonies, but in 1961 India seized Goa, and nationalist movements broke out in Angola and Mozambique: military rule there became increasingly costly, internationally deplored and domestically unpopular.

In 1968 Salazar suffered a stroke and his former protégé Caetano made half-hearted attempts at reform which only inflamed opposition further. Young officers who had grown sympathetic to the causes of the Marxist guerillas they were fighting in Africa formed the Movement of the Armed Forces (MFA) and plotted a coup.

Revolution, Chaos and Recovery

After an abortive attempt, the almost bloodless coup was successfully launched on 25 April 1974, led by General Costa Gomes and General Antonio de Spinola. The people encouraged the move to the left, but general political turmoil led to six provisional governments in two years. The most radical developments occurred in 1975, when private banks and insurance firms were nationalized.

The sudden independence that was given to the colonies caused confusion, too, with civil wars erupting, and almost a million refugees fleeing to Portugal. Their remarkably successful integration into the country has been one of the few triumphs of Portugal's recent history.

After growing disunity both within the MFA and the country as a whole (conservatives in the north, revolutionaries in the south), a radical armed insurrection that broke out in late 1975 was quickly put down by moderate forces under General Ramalho Eanes, thus bringing the revolution to an end.

Eanes was elected President and in 1976 a socialist-influenced Constitution was adopted, with Mário Soares, leader of the Socialist Party, appointed Prime Minister. Over the following years, power swung with familiar instability between the four main parties.

In 1986 veteran socialist leader Mário Soares was elected President (the first civilian Head of State for 60 years), and Cavaco Silva from the right-of-centre Social Democrats became Prime Minister in 1987. Portugal joined the European Community in 1986, a move which is now starting to help the country's ragged infrastructure and industry.

Although still lagging far behind its European neighbours, Portugal's economy has been given a recent boost from foreign investment and tourism. The glorious days of the sea heroes may be over, but the plucky westerners of the Iberian peninsula are now hoping to adapt their traditional penchant for business and trade inland, and establish their niche in a new Europe.

Geography
The 'Garden of Europe'

Sharing only a fifth of the Iberian Peninsula with Spain, Portugal is a small country—about the size of Austria or the American state of Indiana. But it is full of diversity, with 830 kilometres (515 miles) of coastline, high mountain peaks, lush green valleys and flat, dry plains.

The southern Algarve coast boasts the best (and unfortunately most developed) beaches; those exposed to the Atlantic Ocean on the west look lovely, but can be chilly and windswept. Inland, running along the hem of Portugal, the Monchique and Caldeirão mountain ranges act as a minor buffer between the Algarve and the Alentejo plains—a vast, rolling landscape of wheat, cork and olive trees.

Central and northern Portugal, beyond the Tagus River, are dominated by dramatic mountain ranges; Serra da Estrêla has the highest peak, rising to nearly 2,000 metres (6,560 feet). More populated than the south, these central northern areas, particularly the Mondego, Dão and Lima valleys and Douro River wine country, are also considered the country's most scenically beautiful regions. Trás-os-Montes, literally ('behind the mountains') in the remote northeast, is wilder and more rugged, the least developed corner of the land.

The islands of Madeira and the Azores (originally colonized in the fifteenth century and still part of Portugal) are too far from the mainland to be usually included in a peninsular visit: Madeira lies 900 kilometres (559 miles) to the southwest (off the west coast of Africa), while the nine-island archipelago of the Azores are spread in mid-Atlantic about 1,440 kilometres (895 miles) west of Lisbon. Popular destinations in their own right (especially Madeira), these volcanic islands feature a mountainous, verdant landscape, rich in flowers.

Government and Economy
Turmoil and Good Times Ahead

Since the overthrow of the monarchy in 1910, Portugal has been a republic, with an elected president as chief of state and a prime minister who appoints his own cabinet with the president's approval. Members of parliament are elected every four years.

Socialist leader Mário Soares was elected President in 1987. He renounced his Socialist Party ties to cultivate a fatherly image as 'President of all the

Portuguese', and is now the most popular politician in Portugal, affectionately nicknamed 'Uncle Mário'. The Prime Minister, Social Democrat Cavaco Silva, comes a close second in the popularity stakes: his party won 50.2 percent of the vote in the 1987 election. The Socialists remain the second largest party, with 22 percent of the vote, while the tenacious Communist Party (much depleted since the failed 1974 left-wing revolution) retain 12 percent. Despite increasing inflation (up to 12 percent in 1990) and several political scandals, Silva's government is expected to win another term in the 1991 elections.

Portugal joined the European Community in 1986 as the poor man of Europe, its economy and infrastructure in tatters after nearly 50 years of dictatorship and the unstable period of revolutionary chaos. It is now rapidly trying to catch up with its EC partners to meet the demands of the 1992 single market.

With massive financial aid from the EC the country is undergoing a radical transformation; with new roads and office blocks springing up everywhere, the construction business is enjoying an unprecedented boom. So, too, is the economy, currently rated among the fastest growing in the EC: GDP growth reached 5.5 percent in 1989, fixed capital investment grew by 15.5 percent in 1988 (twice the European average) and foreign investment (mostly into real estate and tourism) more than doubled in 1989 to Es.320 billion.

Some of the most dramatic economic changes have been as a result of the government's ambitious privatization programme: the 1975 Constitution was revised in 1989 so that state-run companies expropriated after the 1974 revolution could be sold off. Most of the capital raised is used to reduce the public debt but the opening up of the economy is also encouraging private enterprise and giving new life to the stock exchange.

Industry is also struggling to modernize. Concentrated in three main areas—textiles and clothing, wood and associated products, china and earthenware—it is facing daunting challenges in an increasingly competitive market (most notably from Southeast Asia's textile sector). Agriculture (20 percent of the workforce) has even further to go, with low productivity and often archaic methods.

Undoubtedly, there remain many problems, not least Portugal's chronic trade and public sector deficits and its dependence on unreliable tourism revenues and emigrant worker remittances. But the EC membership has given the country a much-needed boost, and not only financially: for the first time in 500 years the country is looking to Europe. A sense of belonging is growing.

'Our Oldest Ally': Britain and Portugal

Winston Churchill recalled centuries of close liaison when he described Portugal in 1943 as Britain's 'oldest ally'. The first treaty between the two countries was signed in 1373 but ties go back much further, to 1147, when a ruffian band of adventurer-crusaders on their way to the Holy Land were persuaded to stop and help in the reconquest of Lisbon from the Moors. 'Do not be seduced by the desire to press on with your journey,' begged the Bishop of Oporto on behalf of King Afonso Henriques who desperately needed the warriors' help, 'for the praiseworthy thing is not to have been to Jerusalem, but to have lived a good life while on the way.'

It sounded an attractive proposition (the crusaders were offered all the enemy's property if the city were taken) and despite the Moors' contemptuous call from the city walls—'How many times within your memory have you come hither with pilgrims and barbarians to drive us hence?'—the siege was a success.

The crusaders ('plunderers, drunkards and rapists,' exclaimed a contemporary reporter, 'men not seasoned with the honey of piety') duly grabbed their loot and left. But they did leave behind an honourable and intelligent man— Gilbert of Hastings, an English priest, who became the new Bishop of Lisbon.

Further attacks against the Moors by visiting English, Danish and Flemish crusaders followed (their behaviour at Silves was even worse than it had been at Lisbon) until the Pope put a stop to the winter sojourns and encouraged the crusaders on their way to Palestine. Some had enjoyed themselves so much, however, that they settled along the Tagus, thus bringing the first strains of English seafaring blood into the Portuguese race.

In the next century, relations became more genteel, for after English archers helped João I defeat the Castilians at the Battle of Aljubarotta in 1385, thereby securing Portugal's independence, the Treaty of Windsor was signed, declaring perpetual peace and friendship.

The treaty was sealed the following year when João I married Philippa of Lancaster, daughter of John of Gaunt, and sister of the future King Henry IV. The devout and serious Philippa introduced English customs to the Court and English followers to Portugal. Their children (Henry the Navigator was the most famous son) had undeniably English characteristics (Prince Henry was quite unsociable, living like a monk and dying, it is said, a virgin). But the Portuguese took Philippa and her ways to their heart; she was perhaps the most popular Englishwoman ever to grace Portuguese soil.

Another successful royal match between the two countries was made in 1662 when Catherine of Bragança, sister of Dom Afonso VI, married King Charles II. In her turn she introduced novelties to the English court that went down very well, notably tea and toast (the tea parties were useful for keeping her ladies-in-waiting out of her husband's reach). Her dowry gave England some excellent trading perks (including Bombay and Tangier), reinforced in 1703 by the Methuen Treaty. This established the basis of Anglo-Portuguese trade by favouring the sale of English manufactured goods (especially wool) to Portugal in return for providing a market in Britain for Portuguese wines.

England was on to a good thing, and its merchants in Portugal made the best of it, soon dominating the wine trade to the extent that in 1757 the Marquis of Pombal established a company to control all wine production from the Upper Douro. But the economic subservience that the Methuen Treaty had started was not so easily snuffed out. When Napoleon's troops invaded, England came to the rescue but later insisted on the right to trade directly with Brazil. In Portugal's weakened state, it was Marshall Beresford who remained in charge of running the country (the King had fled to Brazil), much as if Portugal was a protectorate of England. It was not a happy moment for England's oldest ally.

But however tense the ties may have occasionally been, they never broke. During the Second World War (when Portugal officially remained neutral) England could count on the use of the Azores for providing facilities for British shipping, an agreement repeated as recently as during the Falklands War.

One can only hope that the Portuguese see the latest invasion of British sunbathers on the Algarve coast as behaving slightly better than their crusading predecessors. But old habits die hard: many Anglo-Saxons decide to stay forever to enjoy the good life in a place that feels, for some strange reason, so much like home.

The Portuguese People
Passion and Patriotism

*Portuguese politeness is delightful, because it is by no means purely artificial,
but flows in a great measure from a natural kindness of feeling.*
(Porchester, later Lord Caernarvon, 1827)

The Portuguese people's friendliness to foreigners is the country's greatest
selling point. As elsewhere in the world, this becomes more striking the further
off the beaten track you go. In the Algarve, I was often politely welcomed and
asked if I was British or German, but in remote Trás-os-Montes villages I was
offered homemade bread and wine and asked to stay for supper.

Striking, too, is the Portuguese people's own passion for their country. 'I love
my land,' declared a dynamic businesswoman with typical frankness. 'I never
want to leave.' Many have done so, of course—mostly villagers from the poorer
northern provinces who first sought their fortunes overseas (in Brazil) during the
eighteenth century. In the 1950s and 60s, emigration to France and Germany
soared (even in the remotest northern areas most villagers speak French).

Although many have returned since the 1980s, some three million Portuguese still live abroad, their remittances bolstering the shaky economy. Other *emigrantes* come back for August holidays to roar around in flashy cars and build bright new houses to replace the family's age-old granite cottage. In some cases, they may return and drift back to their former lifestyles, having succumbed to *saudade*—a uniquely Portuguese emotion of yearning and nostalgia, often related to homesickness.

The variety of the Portuguese people comes as a surprise to visitors, who often expect a Mediterranean-style homogeneity. But the country's many invaders and settlers—from Celts and Carthaginians to Romans and African Muslims—have left traces everywhere: the Portuguese of the north still show Celtic traits, while those of the south reflect their strong Jewish, Moorish and African ancestry. There is a recognized north–south social division, too—the northerners more obviously religious and conservative, more intense than their sunny-climate southern compatriots.

But a sense of warm neighbourliness cossets all towns and villages: conversations are always taking place in the open, on doorsteps, out of windows, across cobbled streets or busy highways, from the back of a mule or an express bus. Talking, in fact, is a popular pastime: *'as palavras sao como as cerejas'* goes a Portuguese saying—words are like cherries, they get so tied up with each other you can't stop them.

You can't rush a Portuguese, either. While the boisterous vitality of the many young people (23 percent of the ten-million population are under the age of 15) gives a dynamic air to Portuguese society, business lifestyle is rather more sedate. Long lunches are taken very seriously. Enjoying life is taken seriously. And for a Portuguese, there is no better place to enjoy it than on home ground.

Food
Bacalhau and the World Beyond

. . . without a shadow of doubt the Portuguese is the most refined, the most voluptuous and succulent cuisine in the world. . . We did acquire—thanks to the spices from the Orient, the tangy bits from Brazil and the art of using sugar from sweet-toothed countries, Turkey, India and the Moors of northern Africa— culinary skills, foods, delicacies, recipes, which turned us into a foremost gastronomic people. There is no other country that can boast such an array of national dishes.

Fialho de Almeida, *Os Gatos*, 1893

To savour the best of Portuguese cuisine you need an adventurous spirit. Despite Senhor Almeida's claims, the voluptuous variety is not always obvious. Portuguese cuisine is basically the simple, honest fare of farmers and fishermen; the surprises are its astonishingly innovative combinations—clams with pork, sausage in soup, trout stuffed with smoked ham—that reflect a spirit as pioneering as that of Portugal's early explorers.

In fact, you can eat your way through Portugal's history from the days of the Romans (they introduced onions, garlic, olives and grapes) to the colonial era (Angola and Brazil brought coffee and the fiery chilli pepper, *piri-piri*, to the Portuguese table, and Indian Goa gave away the secret of its curries). Desserts are very sweet thanks to the Arabs who once dominated the south, cultivating lemon and orange groves, almond and fig trees. Dishes cooked in their *cataplana* invention (a clam-shaped metal pan used for steaming fish, chicken and vegetables) are still the highlight on every Algarve menu.

Other than cinnamon, spices are not as common as one might expect, considering the Portuguese discovered the vital sea route to India and made Lisbon for a time the entrepôt of the spice trade. If anything, it is the tangy olive oil that gives the cuisine its distinctive flavour. The Portuguese love it—they pour it neat over their potatoes and *bacalhau* (salted codfish), and use it liberally in cooking.

Bacalhau is the flagship of Portugal's culinary Age of Discoveries. The first Portuguese codfish fleet is said to have fished off the coast of Newfoundland within years of America's discovery. The sailors salted and sun-dried their catch to make it last the journey home, inventing the uniquely Portuguese *bacalhau* which rivals even fresh fish in local popularity. These days, much of it has to be imported from Norway to meet demand.

Foreigners have a hard time trying to understand the appeal of these hard grey slates of dried fish which double in volume when soaked. There are said to be 365 ways to cook it but the favourite for visitors is the one which disguises its taste most: *bacalhau à Gomes de Sá*—a baked dish including the flaked fish, potatoes and onions, and garnished with hard-boiled eggs and black olives.

Sardines are another matter. Most delicious in summer, they are enjoyed by everyone. Grilled on portable braziers, served with bread, salad and white wine, they epitomize sunny Portuguese seaside holidays. Indeed, fish-lovers are in for the best of times (and not only on the coast), with menus heavily biased towards local fish specialities, as well as nationally popular dishes such as *caldeirada* (fish stew); *arroz de marisco* (seafood paella); *lula grelhado* (grilled squid); *peixe espada* (scabbard fish); *truta* (trout) and *linguado* (sole).

Vegetarians, on the other hand, will wonder why so little of the produce they see in the market ends up on the restaurant table. Perhaps it is because the Portuguese are content with vegetable soups, particularly their beloved *caldo verde*, a jade-green broth of finely-shredded cabbage, potatoes, garlic and occasionally *chouriços* (spicy smoked sausage). A bread-thickened country soup such as *açorda à alentejana* is a meal in itself. And the much-featured *cozido à Portuguesa*, a hotpot of beef, ham, chicken, sausages and vegetables puts new light on the world of stews.

As for meat, the pig is king. Garlicky *salsicha* sausages, *leitão assado* (suckling pig), *presunto* (smoked ham), *rōjoes* (deep-fried nuggets of pork), and above all, *porco à alentejano* (cubes of marinated pork braised with baby clams) are the best of a seemingly never-ending range of pork dishes. Veal steaks are common, too (served with rice, potatoes, French fries, or often all three!), but try *cabrito* (kid), an unexpected delight.

Sobremesas (desserts) are a major menu item. The simplest of them—*pudim de flan* (a firm crème caramel) and *arroz doce* (rice pudding liberally sprinkled with cinnamon)—are sweet enough for most tastes. If not, there is always the well-named saccharine bombshell *pudim molotov*. If you need topping up during the day, head for any *pastelaria* coffee and cake shop, which can offer an assortment of pastries, made with egg yolks and sugar. Nuns of the eighteenth century concocted many of the recipes, giving tongue-in-cheek names to the results, such as *papos de anjo* (angel's breasts) or *barriga de freira* (nun's belly).

You are unlikely to need filling up at the end of a meal, as servings are huge (half-portions are a frequent choice even for adults). But if you want a nibble of cheese, go for the best—*queijo da Serra*, a Brie-like cheese made from pure ewes' milk in the Serra da Estrêla region. Other choices are limited (Portugal's climate is unsuitable for cheese-making) but *queijo da Ilha* (from the Azores) is a popular hard cheese good for picnics, while Alentejo small white creamy cheeses are often served as appetizers (sprinkle them with pepper and salt as the locals do).

The finale, of course, should be coffee and a glass of port: the strong little dose of coffee called a *bica* provides plenty of punch for caffeine addicts. Or you can sip on history with a cup of tea, served rather weak in the style of Catherine of Bragança, who is best remembered not for being the wife of Charles II, but for starting England on its long love affair with tea and toast.

Facts For the Traveller

Visas

Valid passports but no visas are required for British, American, Australian, New Zealand, Canadian, Japanese and European Community citizens for stays of up to 60 days (90 days for Austrians, Australians, French, Italians, Japanese, New Zealanders, Spaniards and Swiss). British Dependent Territories Citizens, British Overseas Citizens and British Nationals (Overseas) must have visas. For longer stays, you can apply for a special visa before you leave or for a further 60-day extension once in Portugal at the Serviços de Estrangeiros (Foreigner's Registration Service), 18 Avenida Antonio Augusto de Aguiar, Lisbon (tel. 01-55047) or its branch offices, located in most major tourist centres.

Getting There

By Air

Portugal's national airline, TAP Air Portugal, has flights to Lisbon from many major cities in Europe, South America and Africa. British Airways, Alitalia, Swissair, Lufthansa, KLM and Air France also provide services from Europe. From the United States (New York, Newark, Boston and Los Angeles), TAP and TWA (from New York only) fly regularly to Lisbon. From Britain, TAP and British Airways fly from London (and TAP only from Dublin and Manchester) to Lisbon, Oporto and Faro. From the Far East the easiest connecting flights to Lisbon are with British Airways, via London, or Lufthansa, via Frankfurt. For Madeira and the Azores, there are flights on TAP from Los Angeles, Boston, and London.

There are also cheap charter flights available from London and several other UK cities, although these are heavily booked during the summer. With over 150 tour operators in the UK offering package tours to Portugal it is often worth investigating other airfare deals that include accommodation and/or car rental. Discount last-minute flights can also be found if you phone travel agents a day before departure. Portugal has no airport tax.

By Rail

A 25-hour train ride on the Sud Express from Paris to Lisbon (return fare little less than an airfare) will probably only appeal to rail enthusiasts or students under 26 able to benefit from reduced-price rail tickets or InterRail passes (EuroRail for Americans and Canadians). The other main rail route into Portugal is from Madrid.

By Boat

There are no direct passenger/car ferry connections between Britain and Portugal—the nearest option goes from Plymouth to Santander in north Spain,

1,080 kilometres (600 miles) from Lisbon. Details from Britanny Ferries (tel. 0752-21321). Some cruise ships call at Lisbon.

By Car

It is a very long drive from Britain/France to Portugal—over 2,000 kilometres (1,200 miles) from the French channel ports to Lisbon. The best solution if you want to take your own car is to go on the car ferry (see above) to Santander in north Spain, or use the convenient (but very expensive) Motorail service between Paris and Lisbon run by French Railways (179 Piccadilly, London Wl, tel. 071-499 9333, SNCF, 88 rue St Lazare, 75436 Paris, Cedex 9, tel. 1-4285 6000). Fly-drive deals and car hire within Portugal (see below) are other possibilities. But a word of warning: although the state of Portugal's roads are improving, driving habits are not—accident rates remain among the worst in Europe. Avoid, if you can, the notoriously dangerous Lisbon–Cascais, Lisbon–Algarve, Lisbon–Oporto and Faro–Portimão highways.

Getting Around

By Air

TAP Air Portugal and its subsidiary, LAR Air Services, have regular flights between Lisbon, Oporto, Faro, Portimão, Covilha, Viseu, and Vila Real.

By Rail

Trains are run by the state-owned Companhia dos Caminhos de Ferro Portugueses (CP) and are good value though not always very convenient or reliable: many railway stations are some distance from the town and nearly all trains are slow *regionais* that stop at practically every station en route. Slightly quicker are the *semi-directos* and *directos*. But the most efficient are the *rápidos* —luxury, expensive trains running between Lisbon–Coimbra–Oporto and Lisbon–Faro. A favourite for business travellers is the airconditioned *Alfa* express which links Lisbon to Oporto in three hours, seven times daily.
After decades of neglect, Portugal's railways and roads are now rapidly being modernized; international high-speed rail links with Spain and a new central station in Lisbon are planned. Deregulation and privatization are on the cards in the race to catch up with the European Community before 1992.
For train buffs and tourists, there have been some tragic results: the wonderful single-track, narrow gauge railways of the north have nearly all been axed as economically unviable. The only one remaining is the Tua Line from Tua to Bragança—and even here, services have been cut back to three a day. Take this incredible ride through the Tua River gorge while it lasts.

By Bus

Travelling by bus is often the quickest and easiest of all public transport options. The national bus company, Rodoviária Nacional (RN) has an extensive network,

and in addition there are many private bus lines operating to smaller towns or on popular routes. Cabanelas Expressos do Nordeste (main terminals at Campo Grande, 30 Lisbon; Rua Ateneu Comercial do Porto, 19 Oporto; Rua D. Pedro de Castro, Vila Real) run an excellent service in the north. For long distance trips, such as between Lisbon and Oporto or Faro, choose an Express RN or private coach, all well advertised at the main bus stations or travel agencies. You can even take a Lisbon or long-range sightseeing tour by bus, with RN Tours (14 Avenida Fontes Pereira de Melo, Lisbon; tel. 01-577523).

By Hire-Car

In addition to the major hire companies (Hertz, Avis, Europcar, etc.) found at the airports and leading hotels, there are local companies in the major cities which offer cheaper rates. In high season a week's hire with a major company will cost at least Es.50,000 (see Money, page 41 for approximate exchange rates); this gives you unlimited mileage, and includes insurance, government tax, and collision damage waiver. Petrol in 1989 was Es. 130 a litre. It is often cheaper for British visitors to arrange car hire at home before departure.

Portugal's roads are undergoing major improvements; thanks largely to massive EEC grants, some Es.72 billion a year is being spent on new highways and on re-surfacing and re-cobbling old roads. But they have a long way to go: even in the Algarve conditions are still terrible. Expect potholes everywhere!

Climate

The best time to visit is between April and November, although you can nearly always find sunshine in the Algarve where temperatures rarely drop below 13°C (55°F) and reach a high of 24°C (75°F) in summer. Lisbon has an average annual temperature of 16°C (62°F) but nights can be cool even in summer, and in winter it is rainy and cold. Further north, in the mountains, it can get even colder (snow falls in winter on the Serra da Estrêla mountains). Summer temperatures in the Oporto region rise to about 20°C (68°F). Bring an umbrella for autumn or early spring visits to the green and well-soaked Minho province.

Health

No special vaccinations are required, although a cholera-typhoid jab would be an extra precaution. It is advisable to take out medical insurance as there is no free medical treatment for foreigners. Local chemists *(farmácia)* have highly trained pharmacists able to dispense drugs (some on prescription only) for minor problems. In more serious cases you can usually find an English-speaking doctor (many Portuguese doctors were trained in the UK or USA). Lisbon has a British Hospital (49 Rua Saraiva de Carvalho, tel. 01-602020) with a staff of English-speaking doctors and nurses. In emergencies, dial 115.

Money

The Portuguese currency unit is the escudo, divided into 100 centavos. Its symbol, the $ sign, is written between the escudo and centavo units (e.g. 50$00 is 50 escudos; 50$50 is 50 escudos and 50 centavos). One thousand escudos is known as a *conto*. The banks are open 8.30 am to 3 pm, Monday to Friday and are the best places to change money: they nearly all accept travellers' cheques (although charging a hefty commission fee). Outside of banking hours, some central branches in Lisbon and Oporto and currency exchanges at airports stay open till late (e.g. Lisbon's Banco Borges at Praça dos Restauradores is open until 7 pm). Major credit cards are accepted in the more expensive shops, hotels, and restaurants. But stock up on cash if you are going into remoter areas. Exchange rates are roughly Es.150 to the US$, Es.250 to the £, and Es.30 to the French franc. Note that most accommodation costs and entrance fees rise steeply in high season (June or July to September).

Communications

Post offices are open from Monday to Friday, 9 am to 6 pm. In addition to postal, telegram and telephone services the main post offices in large towns and major hotels also have telefax machines. New-style street pay phones (easier to use than the old ones) have instructions written in English and can take international calls, though it is far easier to go to the main post office (and cheaper than in your hotel).

Opening Hours

Officially, shops and businesses operate from 9 am to 5 pm, but in practice most open nearer 10 am, close for a long lunch break and siesta (usually 12.30 pm to 2.30 pm) and stay open until 6 pm or 7 pm. Not many businesses are open after 1 pm on a Saturday.

Entertainment

In Lisbon all **nightlife** centres round the restaurants in Bairro Alto where there is everything from gay bars to rock bands, the sober Port Wine Institute to late-night performances of *fado*—the haunting, lyrical laments that are sung to a 12-string guitar accompaniment (see Music and Maps page 45).

The best places to hear *fado* are traditional bars called *casas de fado* or *adegas típicas*. The singing starts late—about 10 pm—and can go on until the early hours. Most of these *fado* restaurants now have a fairly high entrance charge (at least Es.1,500 per person) and some are geared very much to tourist gimmicks rather than to the quality of the music. Among the more reputable (and expensive) *fado* houses are **Senhor do Vinho**, 18 Rua do Meio à Lapa

(tel. 01-672681);
A Severa, 55 Rua das Gaveas
(tel. 01-364006); and
Recordação de Lisboa, 54 Rua
da Barroca (tel. 01-326742).

In **Coimbra**, which has
another, more intellectual
version of *fado*, two of the best
fado restaurants are **Trovador**,
Largo da Sé (tel. 039-25475),
and **Diligência**, 30 Rua Nova
(tel. 039-27667). **BoemiaBar** in
6 Rua do Cabido (tel. 039-
34547) has popular Portuguese
music. Be sure to check with the
Turismo office on times of
performances at all these
restaurants.

Musical entertainment is not
limited just to *fado*. Lisbon has a
lively **jazz, rock and African
music** scene—check out
Gafiera, Calcada de Tijolo (tel.
01-325953) for Brazilian sambas, **Lontra**, Rua de São Bento (tel. 01-661083)
for Cape Verde bands and **Hot Clube de Portugal**, Praça da Alegria, for the
latest jazz sounds. **Fragil** at 128 Rua da Atalaia (tel. 01-369528) is the liveliest
disco in town.

Major **classical music concerts** throughout Portugal are often sponsored by
the Gulbenkian Foundation; the Turismo office will have details. A summer
festival of music takes place in Sintra. **Films** are a great bargain: for less than
Es.500 you can see the latest British, American or European movies in their
original languages (with Portuguese subtitles).

Gamblers will be happy in the **casinos** in the Algarve (Alvor, Monte Gordo,
Vilamoura), in Estoril, Figueira da Foz, Póvoa de Varzim and Espinho. Lottery
tickets are sold on the streets everywhere.

Bullfights may hardly fit some people's idea of entertainment, but the
bullfights in Portugal are different from those in Spain: here, the bull is not
killed (at least, not in the ring). And most of the bullfight takes place on horse-
back. In fact, it is a very refined affair altogether, with a mounted *cavaleiro* in
elegant eighteenth-century costume skilfully evading the bull while trying to
plant a dart into its neck. This accomplished, a team of eight *forcados* moves in

on foot, taunting the bull and wrestling it with their bare hands. The men inevitably fare far worse than the bull.

The best place to see genuine Portuguese bullfights is in the Ribatejo province where the bulls are bred; from April to October, most festivals here will feature a bullfight. In Lisbon, bullfights take place regularly at Campo Pequeno.

Sports

Football fans will be relieved to know the sport is very much alive and kicking in Portugal. The three major teams (Benfica and Sporting from Lisbon; FC Porto from Oporto, the 1987 European champions) have a passionate, nationwide following, as you will soon discover during the September to May football season, when all restaurant televisions tune in to the latest match. Tickets are inexpensive, but difficult to get for the big three—try the ticket kiosk in Lisbon's Praça dos Restauradores.

Golf has long been a hot favourite here: the Oporto Golf Club established a course in 1890. There are now 17 courses, all but six of world championship standard and designed by international experts such as Henry Cotton, Frank Pennink and Robert Trent Jones. Most of the best are in the Algarve, including the renowned Vale do Lobo and Quinta do Lago courses, but there are also courses near Lisbon (Estoril and Cascais), and in Oporto, Vidago, and Sétubal.

As you would expect, **watersports** are best in the Algarve, although you can also find good windsurfing at Guincho, on the Estoril coast. The slickest **tennis** facilities are also in the Algarve (Penina, Quinta do Lago, Vilamoura, etc.), with courts elsewhere in the country attached to sports clubs.

Shopping

If you arrive in Portugal from Spain you might well think the only thing for sale in the country are cheap towels, T-shirts, and linen. But beyond the frontier and the needs of Spanish day-trippers you will soon discover a variety of handicrafts.

In the **Algarve**, pottery, wickerwork or even an intricate Algarvian chimney (good as lampshades) are tempting buys. Further north, in the **Alentejo**, keep your eye out for beautifully painted furniture, rugs from Arraiolas (pricey) or bizarre little earthenware figurines from Estremoz. **Lisbon** and **Oporto** are the places to find good bargains in gold and silver filigree jewellery, leather goods, and linen.

More expensive buys are the famous porcelain of Vista Alegre, tapestries, and *azulejo* tiles in modern styles. In **Óbidos**, exquisitely embroidered linen is available in many of the little shops, while nearby **Caldas da Rainha** sells the popular cabbage-leaf pottery. In the **Minho** and **Douro** provinces you can go wild at big local fairs such as **Barcelos** on pottery and rural novelties, including carved wooden ox-yokes, wine barrels, straw hats and saddles. Even in the remotest corners of **Trás-os-Montes** you will come across unique handicrafts, such as little penknives from **Palacoulo** and silk cushion covers from **Freixo de Espada-à-Cinta.**

Music

Music in Portugal ranges from traditional harvest songs to the latest Angolan rock. At local festivals you can hear songs and instrumental music whose origins can be traced back to the days of Provençal troubadours. Many regional groups have made cassettes of their performances which are on sale at fairs, markets and in local shops; the Alentejo groups are particularly good.

But above all it is *fado* which has become internationally famous. A sad, lyrical lament which emerged in the eighteenth century, it first became popular in Lisbon's Alfama district. Another, more intellectual version from the northern university city of Coimbra is still performed by the students. But both specialize in sentiment, bordering on pessimism (the name *fado* is said to come from the Latin *fatum*, meaning destiny).

The unrivalled star of *fado* is Amália Rodrigues, though she rarely performs nowadays. Pick up her 'Greatest Hits' (released in 1986) for an idea of what *fado* should really sound like. Other *fado* names to look out for are Carlos do Carmo, Alberto Prado and Castro Rodrigo.

Groups from Portugal's former African colonies are providing the most exciting sounds nowadays in jazz and rock. From Guiné Bissau, some of the big names are Justinio Delgado, Manecas and Africa Libre; from southern Africa, Fernando Luís and Guem. You can pick up records or cassettes of all these groups at good prices. For Portuguese rock music, which flourished after the Revolution, try Rui Veloso, who started the whole thing going.

Maps

Michelin and Lascelles produce a good overall edition, though the best road map is by the Automovel Clube de Portugal, available at 49A Avenida Rosa Araújo, Lisbon. Detailed, up-to-date walking maps are non-existent and your best bet is to get a Portuguese friend to buy you an out-dated army map (not sold to foreigners) available at the Serviços Cartograficos do Execito, Avenida Dr Alfredo Bensaúde, Olivais Norte, Lisbon; or at Porta Editora, Rua da Fábrica, Oporto.

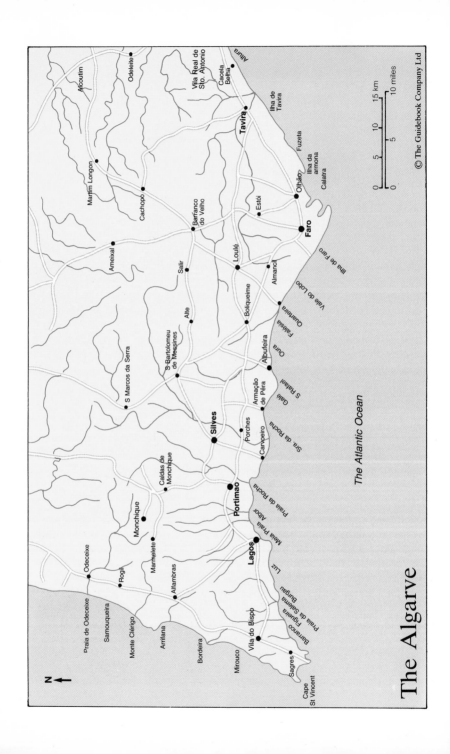

The Algarve

N

The Atlantic Ocean

© The Guidebook Company Ltd

| 0 | 5 | 10 | 15 km |

| 0 | 5 | 10 miles |

Alcoutim

Odeleite

Vila Real de Sto. António

Altura

Cacela Belha

Tavira

Ilha de Tavira

Martim Longon

Cachopô

Barranco do Velho

Fuzeta

Ilha da armona

Calatra

Olhão

Ameixal

Salir

Loulé

Estói

Faro

Almancil

Ilha de Faro

Alte

Boliqueime

Vale do Lobo

S Marcos da Serra

S Bartolomeu de Messines

Albufeira

Falésia

Quarteira

Oura

S Rafael

Gaiè

Silves

Armação de Péra

Caldas de Monchique

Porches

Carvoeiro

Sra. da Rocha

Monchique

Portimão

Praia da Rocha

Odeceixe

Rogil

Marmelete

Alfambras

Lagos

Mela Praia

Meia Praia Albor

Luz

Praia de Odeceixe

Samouqueira

Monte Clérigo

Arrifana

Bordeira

Mirouco

Vila do Bispo

Burgau

Praia da Salema

Figueira

Barranco

Sagres

Cape St Vincent

The South

The Algarve

Only 30 years ago few people had even heard of the Algarve. Portugal's southernmost province—the last part of the country to be wrested from the Moors in 1249—is now its most famous, thanks to that infallible tourist formula of sun, sand and sea, set against an appealing landscape of citrus groves and flowers, low, white-washed houses and pretty Moorish fishing villages. Tourism first began to take off in the 1960s after the opening of Faro airport. While building restrictions were in force the coast remained relatively unscathed, with the emphasis on a few golf courses and luxury hotels among the pine forests. But after the 1974 revolution, the controls collapsed, and mass tourism was encouraged. The Algarve today suffers only too obviously from the results: hideous high-rise apartment blocks, overcrowded resorts, polluted seas, and one of the most dangerous highways in Europe.

That is the bad news. The good news is that not all of the 270-kilometre (167-mile) southern coastline is a disaster zone. West of Lagos and east of Faro you can still find bays and beaches with scarcely a sunburnt tourist in sight. And not all resorts are awful: those which have maintained their up-market approach, such as Vale do Lobo, have been built to blend in with their surroundings, and offer superb facilities, including some of the best golf courses in Europe.

Inland, too, in the foothills of the Serras de Monchique and do Caldeirão— the mountains dividing the Algarve from neighbouring Alentejo province—are hidden rural gems largely ignored by the suntan-seeking hordes.

The Algarve's rapid development may well be its downfall: in the past few years some ten percent of the region's 1.5 million British tourists have voted with their feet and gone elsewhere. This may stave off any further unsightly coastal development, although new resorts for 'quality tourism' are now creeping inland.

For those who want to collapse on a beach with all facilities provided and guaranteed sunshine, the Algarve can still offer one of the best deals in Europe. But if you want culture and Portuguese atmosphere, then head north.

Faro

The capital of the Algarve since 1756, Faro is known to most visitors today because of its international airport, six kilometres (four miles) from the centre of town. The journey in (Es.800 by taxi, or take bus no. 18 or 16) past messy construction sites does not inspire confidence, but the town is better than you might expect. Cobbled streets of pastel-coloured houses fan out from a little yacht harbour where young Africans set up stalls of leather and jewellery. Choose a place like the café in the middle of Praça Ferreira de Almeida to acclimatize. Portuguese men gather here to gossip and drink the Algarve wine, oblivious to the tourists milling around.

Faro's list of sights is short: several major disasters—a sacking by the Earl of Essex in 1596 and the great earthquake of 1755—have left few major monuments. But it does have a small and peaceful semi-walled **old quarter** entered through the eighteenth-century **Arco da Vila** (formerly a castle gate) next to the **Turismo** (8 Rua da Misericordia). A spacious cobbled square in the centre is flanked by the bishop's palace and **Cathedral**, a mix of Gothic, Renaissance and Baroque styles. The most eye-catching item inside is the fancy organ.

Around the corner is the **Archaeological Museum** (open Monday to Friday, 9 am–noon, 2–5 pm) in a sixteenth-century convent. The rooms around the cloister contain local Roman remains including an impressive third-century pavement mosaic of Neptune that once lay along Faro's Rua Infante de Henrique. Upstairs are *azulejos* (glazed tiles), woodcuts, and an eclectic private collection that ranges from Rembrandts to jasper ash-trays.

The **Regional Ethnographic Museum** (Rua do Pé da Cruz; open Monday to Friday, 9.30 am–12.30 pm, 2–5 pm) is a nostalgic place. See pre-tourism Algarve here in black-and-white photos and dioramas. There is also a striking model of the huge net system once used to catch tuna (called a *madrague*) though the best fish, boat and net displays are in the small **Maritime Museum** by the harbour (open Monday to Friday, 9.30 am–12.30 pm, 2–5.30 pm, Saturday 9.30 am–1 pm; closed Sunday). Unusually, there are good captions in both English and French.

'Stop here and think of this fate that will befall you' commands the sign above the entrance to the macabre **Capela de Ossos** (Chapel of Bones), behind the baroque **Carmo Church** (Largo do Carmo). Built in 1816 from the surrounding monastic cemetery, its walls are covered with 1,245 skulls interlaced with elbow bones and tibia. 'See! Here is a skull with a complete set of teeth!' says the custodian merrily. Snapshots with your favourite bone are apparently OK: a Fuji advertisement is stuck on the altar. Those with ghoulish tastes may note that there is an even bigger Capela de Ossos in Évora.

West of Faro

From Faro all the way to Lagos, the coastline is packed with resorts and **luxury holiday villages** such as Quinta do Lago, Vale do Lobo, Quarteira, and Vilamoura (roughly in that order of elegance and increasing ugliness).

An incongruous gem amidst the development is in the hamlet of **Almancil**, off the main road 13 kilometres (eight miles) northwest of Faro. The interior of the **Church of São Lourenço** is completely covered with *azulejos* by Policarpo de Oliveira, dating from 1730. There is no better place for an introduction to these ubiquitous glazed tiles. In a converted cottage down the lane, the **São Lourenço Culture Centre** displays Algarvian arts and crafts.

Some 26 kilometres (16 miles) further west, **Albufeira** was a prosperous trading port under the Moors. Now it trades in tourists: it is one of the Algarve's most popular package tour destinations. Not much is left of its old character but one area around **Rua da Igreja Velha** still has Moorish arches and tiny cobbled lanes which are worth exploring.

Carvoeiro, 12 kilometres (seven miles) before Portimão, is an intimate little place out-of-season with an atmospheric mix of new, old and ruined houses; but its tiny beach cannot cope with crowds. As for **Portimão,** one of the largest and ugliest towns on the coast, its only attraction (aside from the development which looms above) is the **Praia da Rocha**, with its famous rock formations. But don't expect to find a patch of sand to yourself.

The huge (but shadeless) beach at nearby **Alvor** might be a better bet; this old port at the mouth of the Alvor estuary is an undeveloped spot which has kept the high-rise holiday flats at bay. Dazzling white houses and friendly al fresco restaurants maintain Alvor's precarious charm.

Lagos is a different kettle of fish entirely. Now totally dedicated to tourism (a more cosmopolitan and up-market kind than at Albufeira), its cove beaches with their curious grottoes are an Algarve speciality, particularly the **Praia Dona Ana**. The town itself has been popular for a long time: Phoenicians, Carthaginians, Romans and Moors all settled here, and during the fifteenth-century Age of Discoveries, Prince Henry the Navigator used it as a base for expeditions round the coast of Africa. You can still see the site of the **slave market** under the arches of the former Customs House in Praça da República, where the first slaves from Africa were sold.

Within the old town walls, the narrow, steep streets are a driver's nightmare and a stroller's delight. In Rua Marreiros Nello, near the **Turismo** (Praça M. de Pombal), homesick Brits head for Borley's, 'British butcher, sausage and pie man', selling Cornish pasties and apple pies just like mum makes them at home.

The **Municipal Museum** (open 9.30 am–12.30 pm, 2.30–5.30 pm; closed Monday), attached to the **Church of Santo Antonio** (Rua General Alberto Silveira) is one of the best museums in the Algarve. Bigger inside than it first appears, it is crammed with oddities ranging from wax dolls to sacred art and old surgical instruments to preserved animal freaks (two-headed kitten, eight-legged goat). The highlight, though, is the baroque church itself, laden with gilt woodwork carved around 1715.

Between Lagos and Cape St Vincent—the southwestern corner of Portugal and of continental Europe—development gradually disappears and you find life pretty much as it always has been: horses ploughing the fields, women in thick woollen stockings walking the roads with pails balanced on their heads, and unspoilt villages perched by the seashore. Try **Salema** or even better, **Praia da Ingrina**, for places with minimum tourist facilities.

Vila do Bispo, en route for Sagres, and surrounded by fields, has a curiously

Luís de Camões and the National Epic

'This is the story of heroes who, leaving their native Portugal behind them, opened a way to Ceylon, and further, across seas no man had ever sailed before. They were men of no ordinary stature, equally at home in war and in dangers of every kind: they founded a new kingdom among distant peoples, and made it great.'

So begins *Os Lusiadas (The Lusiads)*, the epic poem by Luís Vaz de Camões named after the sons of Lusus, companion of Bacchus and mythical first settler of Portugal. Ostensibly, the poem relates the historic sea voyage by Vasco da Gama to India in 1497. But like Homer's Odyssey, it is more than just a story: it is a song of praise to the greatness of the Portuguese spirit, written at a time when Portugal was still (though not for much longer) one of the richest and most powerful countries in the Western world. When it was first published in 1572, the poem received few plaudits, although it was sufficiently recognized for its poetic and patriotic worth to help Camões win a small royal pension. Over 400 years later, it is considered the national epic, its poet a national hero.

Camões enjoyed little fame or fortune while he was alive. Reflecting the theme of his poem, his life was full of struggles and vicissitudes—or so it is generally believed: romantic guesswork has been woven into the few hard facts available. Born probably in 1524 (the same year, incidentally, that Vasco da Gama died) to an impoverished aristocratic family, he is said to have spent his happiest years at the University in Coimbra where he would have received a thorough grounding in Latin, Greek and European literature. But after moving to Lisbon in 1544 where he mixed in Court and aristocratic circles, writing poetry and plays, he got himself into trouble by having an affair with one of the Queen's ladies-in-waiting.

Banished from the capital, his life suddenly shifted dramatically. In 1547 he went to serve in North Africa as a soldier and lost his right eye. By the time he returned to Lisbon two years later, he had changed from a studious romantic to a tougher man altogether. In 1552 he was involved in a street brawl and wounded a royal official. First imprisoned, he was later released on condition he went to serve in India. He arrived in Goa in 1553 and later served in Macau, losing everything in a shipwreck except his life and the half-completed manuscript of his epic poem.

After six more years in Goa (including a couple of spells in prison for unknown misdemeanours), Camões was obviously keen to return home. But he only had enough money to reach Mozambique where he languished for another couple of years before finally returning to Lisbon in 1570. It had been 17 years since he had seen his motherland.

Much had changed. Not least, it was obvious Portugal was losing its grip on its empire, and heading for disaster. 'This country of mine is made over to lusting greed,' Camões wrote at the end of *The Lusiads,* 'its sense of values eclipsed in an austerity of gloom and depression: there is no longer to be had from it that recognition which fans the flame of genius as nothing else can.'

The young and recklessly idealistic Dom Sebastiao had just taken the throne, intent on reviving the crusading ideals of Afonso V and conquering Morocco. He set out in 1578 with a force of 18,000 in 500 ships. In a devastating battle, the king and most of Portugal's nobility were killed. Only 100 escaped capture. It was the beginning of the end for Portugal, and Camões knew it.

'All will see,' he wrote on his deathbed. 'that so dear to me was my country I was content to die not only in but with it.' He had no heirs; no wife, no siblings. And so little money he was buried in a common grave. Only after his death was his genius truly recognized; a vast body of his lyric poetry was posthumously published and the influence of his work on both Portuguese and Brazilian literature soon came to be unrivalled.

Three hundred years after his death, what were believed to be his remains were moved to Jerónimos Monastery, that supreme expression of confidence in the Age of Discoveries, built on the spot from which Vasco da Gama had sailed to India in 1497. Camões' recumbent figure in stone was crowned with laurel leaves. And across the chancel, a few steps away, was placed the tomb of his hero, Vasco da Gama.

remote air. Few travellers stop here, but the church is an unexpected treat, with a painted ceiling, heavily-gilt side chapels and a treasure trove of embroidered vestments and sixteenth-century paintings. Outside, the locals sit on the church wall and watch the world pass by to Sagres.

In fact, it is not Sagres village itself (which is nothing special) that draws visitors but its history: at **Sagres** ('where the land ends and the sea begins', wrote Luís de Camões) Prince Henry the Navigator founded his School of Navigation, a fifteenth-century mariners' think-tank to work out a sea route to India, and set up shipyards to build the caravels that were to take his explorers into the unknown world.

An imposing eighteenth-century fortress on a windswept plateau beyond the village encloses a fourteenth-century chapel and what some say is the Prince's former residence (now a very spartan youth hostel). But the most interesting item—in front of the hostel and almost covered by weeds—is a huge pebble wind compass, perhaps also used by the Prince.

Six kilometres (four miles) further west is **Cape St Vincent**, 75 metres (246 feet) above the ocean and a place of eerie isolation. Here stand a lighthouse, the ruins of a sixteenth-century Capuchin convent, and fishermen silently dangling lines down into the depths below.

East of Faro

The large fishing port of **Olhão**, eight kilometres (five miles) east of Faro, tucks an attractive old quarter of Moroccan-style 'cubist' white houses within a duller modern town. The Pensão Bicuar or the bell-tower of the **parish church** (built in the 17th century with donations from fishermen) are the two best places to view the old town. Note the distinctive Olhão chimneys—simple and square, with no lace-like decoration.

The waterfront market is great fun in the early morning, and several restaurants along this main Avenue 5 de Outubro offer excellent fish menus (try no. 58 for its squid kebabs). But it is offshore that Olhão keeps its best secret: a series of *ilhas*, sandbank islands including Ilha da Armona and Culatra which offer simple chalet accommodation and deserted beaches. Ferries leave from the jetty just before the port at least nine times a day in high season to Armona (the preferable choice), eight times a day to Culatra.

Tavira, 30 kilometres (19 miles) east of Faro, is the saving grace of the Algarve coast. A beautiful town that has somehow escaped development, it stretches either side of the Rio Gilao, with old houses and fishing boats lined up along the quay (tuna-fishing was once its major industry), and a park of palm trees, craft stalls and cafés. Churches are chock-a-block in Tavira; the hilltop **Church of Santa Maria do Castelo** dominates them all, a Gothic structure built on the site of a former mosque.

Only the walls remain from the nearby **castle**, given a facelift by Dom Dinis in the thirteenth century, but there are good views of the town from the corner turrets, where lovers like to nest. The **bridge** across the river was once part of the Roman road linking Faro and Mértola (though Tavira's origins go back much further, to at least 400 BC when the Greeks settled here).

Twenty-three kilometres (14 miles) east of Tavira, the dreary eighteenth-century frontier town of **Vila Real de Santo Antonio** has little to recommend it other than an interesting way out—by boat up the River Guadiana. **River cruises** leave Thursday and Sunday for a day's excursion including barbecue and a stop at a hotel's swimming pool. Tickets are available from the **Turismo** here (off Avenida da República) and in Tavira. A bridge over the river to Spain will soon provide an overland route east; currently ferries make the link every half-hour until 11 pm.

Inland

The twisting mountain road from Odeleite, 30 kilometres (19 miles) north of Vila Real de Santo Antonio, to **Alcoutim** is one of the most dramatic in the Algarve: it follows the River Guadiana past villages right on the water's edge. Alcoutim's fourteenth-century castle boldly faces its Spanish counterpart, the rather more imposing castle of Sanlucar del Guadiana. You can brush up your Spanish by listening to voices from its surrounding village.

Aside from a rash of new houses to the northwest, Alcoutim is rural Algarve at its best: cobbled lanes, white-washed houses, pretty chimneys, and surrounding hills without another town in sight. It seems appropriate that an important peace treaty between Castile and Portugal was signed here in 1371, on garlanded boats anchored in the river.

Some 16 kilometres (ten miles) northwest of Faro, **Loulé** makes a good day's outing from the coast, its charming old walled town featuring the ruins of a thirteenth-century castle and winding lanes with some bizarre contrasts: at the village font, dated 1837, old women still do their laundry while the young use the water to clean their cars.

One of the best things about **Silves**, 28 kilometres (17 miles) northwest of Albufeira, is the view of its castle from a distance, perched above a valley of fruit orchards. Ironically, considering the ruffian behaviour of the English crusaders who helped sack Silves in 1189 when it was the capital of the Moors, there is a Café Ingles in the shadow of the castle, and an English-style telephone box by the nearby thirteenth-century cathedral. You can conjure up the crusaders' exploits as you walk the castle's chunky red walls.

Caldas de Monchique, 22 kilometres (14 miles) northwest of Silves, is an Algarve gem, a Victorian spa with faded mansions set among hills of eucalyptus. A night at the rambling Central Pensão, with its bare floorboards, bowls of greenery and wandering Afghan hound is guaranteed to be memorable.

Seven kilometres (four miles) further north, and 200 metres (656 feet) higher in the Serra de Monchique, is **Monchique** itself, an odd little place rescued just in time—or so it seems—from completely fading away. Have a look at the strange knotted Manueline doorway of the church, striking against the white-washed façade.

Off the Track

The west coast of the Algarve has hardly been touched by tourism, probably because the sea is cold and often rough. But the **Praia de Odeceixe** is a secluded cove, with only a few villas on the cliffs. In the village, three kilometres (less than two miles) away, are rooms to rent and a couple of shops. If you are heading south, look out for a beautiful, abandoned windmill just after Rogil, set in a meadow of wild lilies.

Cacela Velha is something of a miracle: on the southern coast just eight kilometres (five miles) east of Tavira, it has not only kept the tourists away but also most of the twentieth century. There are no shops, no hotels and just two tiny bar/restaurants. Surrounded by vineyards, almond and olive groves, it is perched high above the sea, with a view right out to the Spanish border. Its cottages cluster round a small seventeenth-century fort (now a Guarda Fiscal post), and a sixteenth-century church. Mobile vans bring afternoon groceries, drawing the women from their doorways. Otherwise, not much happens: seagulls swoop around the cliffs, out to the offshore sandbank, while a villager potters in his vegetable plot below the castle walls, and the grapes grow a little riper.

The Alentejo

This huge province south of the River Tagus covers nearly a third of the country and stretches from the Spanish border to the Atlantic Ocean. It is distinguished by its rolling plains of wheatfields and cork-oak trees, large farms and burning summers. Most of its interest lies in the north which includes the historical city of Évora and the hilltop fortresses of Marvão and Monsaraz. But even the expansive southern plains have a simple, rural beauty, and the coastal area holds a host of secrets.

The Alentejo provides the world with half of its cork supply and the country with its most innovative pork dish (*porco à Alentejano*—marinaded cubes of pork braised with clams). But it remains an impoverished and underpopulated province. After the 1974 Revolution, landless workers seized the estates of rich landowners to set up hundreds of co-operatives; many failed since responsibility tended to go to the best communists rather than the most competent farmers. The last co-operatives were shut down at the end of 1989 by the new centre-right government, and farms are now being returned to the former landowners or sold to foreign agri-businesses.

Public transport is limited; Évora, Beja and Portalegre are your best bets for train and bus connections. Beyond the main cities, good accommodation is sparse. But the Alentejo's hinterland, with its slow pace and warm-hearted locals, more than makes up in character what it lacks in facilities.

Baixa (Lower) Alentejo

The most notable town in this region is **Beja**, called Pax Julia by the Romans after peace was made by Julius Caesar with the Lusitani tribe, and now a sizeable agricultural centre (mainly for wheat and olive oil) with a pleasant old quarter. In the seventeenth-century Beja won fame as a result of some scandalous love letters addressed to a French cavalry officer, allegedly written by a nun from the town's **Convento de NS da Conçeicão.**

The convent, dissolved with all other religious orders in 1834, is now the **Regional Museum** (open 10 am–1 pm, 2.30–5 pm, closed Sunday), and the main place to head for. Its gilded chapel leads on to a cloister whose four sides or 'courts' are decorated in different styles of *azulejos*. The chapter house has some remarkable sixteenth-century Moorish tiles (with their tight multicoloured patterns quite different from later Portuguese ones) and a flamboyant painted ceiling. Upstairs, romantics can see the grill-window through which the nun and her lover whispered endearments.

The **castle** (open 10 am–1 pm, 2–6 pm) is worth a quick look; one of Dom Dinis' many castle creations, it has a massive keep with Gothic windows. On Saturdays, a market spreads around the walls, full of black-hatted gentlemen and full-skirted gypsy women.

The Art of Azulejos

If there is one thing that distinguishes Portugal's churches, palaces, stations and parks from those of other European countries, it is the unrestrained use of *azulejos*—blue and white or polychrome wall tiles.

Portugal's unrivalled passion for these glazed tiles began over 500 years ago. The Moors had already introduced a geometric style of *azulejos* into the country (for instance, in the Royal Palace at Sintra) but after the Portuguese captured Ceuta in 1415, they began to discover *azulejos* for themselves in Morocco and to make their own, mainly blue ('azul') tiles.

At this time, colours were separated by strokes of linseed oil or manganese, but in the sixteenth century the Italians invented the majolica technique, which enabled colours to be painted directly onto the wet clay, over a layer of white enamel. It gave the Portuguese the springboard they needed, and the *azulejo* craze began.

Initially, the designs closely resembled carpet or tapestry patterns, and often covered whole walls or altar fronts in a variety of colours, predominantly yellow and blue. The overseas explorations of the time also led to some exotic Indo-Portuguese features such as a plethora of animals, flowers and birds. But an even stronger influence was the European fashion for blue and white Chinese porcelain, which had been imported into Europe by the Portuguese in the early sixteenth century. Blue and white earthenware tiles invented in Delft successfully exploited the craze and soon the interest in multicoloured tiles began to wane.

But not before the Portuguese had gone a step further with their multicoloured designs; in the late seventeenth century they started to introduce narrative and lifestyle scenes—panels showing hunting, fishing or harvesting gatherings, landscapes, picnics and all sorts of jollities, later inspired by the bucolic paintings of eighteenth-century French artists such as Watteau and Fragonard. Every nobleman had to have his *azulejo* hunting panel, every church its life of Christ or the saints.

These narrative tiles enjoyed their heyday in the eighteenth century when such masters as Antonio de Oliveira Bernardes produced brilliant sweeps of *azulejos*, perfectly complementing their surroundings (as in Évora's Lóios Church). Bernardes and his son Policarpo set up an *azulejos* school in Lisbon that was to greatly influence the development of the art in Portugal. It was at this time that life-size doormen became popular in *azulejo* panels in manor houses—static butlers in blue and white, conveniently always on duty.

With industrial manufacture (and the rapid need for huge quantities of *azulejos* after the 1755 earthquake), quality began to suffer. But the fashion never disappeared. Polychrome *azulejos* took on a rococo flavour, decorating fountains, stairways (as in Lamego's Church of N S dos Remedios) and even kitchens. Later still, plain-coloured tiles adorned the facades of houses, adding a glow of elegance (Andre Soares da Silva's blue-fronted Casa do Raio in Braga is a beautiful example).

Azulejos have their place in twentieth-century Portuguese art, too—Maria Keil, a leading tile artist, made a striking wall mural in Lisbon in the 1960s. If you are interested in seeing more examples, and tracing the history and technique of *azulejos* over the ages, visit Lisbon's excellent Museu do Azulejo in the Convent of Madré

The approach from Beja to **Serpa**, 28 kilometres (17 miles) to the southeast, is very striking, the crenellated walls of a thirteenth-century castle vying for attention with an eleventh-century aqueduct. Nearly everything about Serpa seems elegant; even the door-knockers are impressive.

You will probably get bombed by swallows on the walls of the **castle**, but it is worth it for the views of the terracotta-tiled town and the plains beyond. The **Archaeological Museum** here has Visigothic, Roman and Muslim remains, and an incongruous larger-than-lifesize diorama of the Last Supper. The **Ethnographic Museum** (Largo do Corro, open Tuesday to Saturday, 9–noon, 2–6 pm) contains a stylish display of local craftsmen's tools and costumes.

58 kilometres (36 miles) northeast of Beja, **Moura** boasts a *poco arabe* (little Arabia) quarter of low, white-washed houses. No. 11 Travessa da Mouraria has been turned into a tiny **Islamic Museum** with some pottery fragments and Moorish stone tablets. Inside the cottage at no. 4 an old man makes coloured wire baskets.

More evidence of the Moors is found in **Mértola**, 50 kilometres (31 miles) south of Beja, above the River Guadiana. The old walled town has a remote and mysterious air; few tourists come here. The thirteenth-century **castle** ruins dominate the warren of streets where women sit crocheting on their doorsteps, some wearing black trilby hats like the men. Painted carts are parked nearby, wheels braked with slate.

The thirteenth-century square **church** is a rare example of a former mosque (its curious Gothic door carved with men, babies and lions). Seats inside are arranged in a semi-circle, among a dozen Moorish columns, and the *mihrab* (prayer niche) remains visible behind the altar. The **Museum** in the old town hall below displays its Roman foundations with atmospheric lighting, making the most of a few pots and shards and headless goddesses. A little further along the lane a small **Islamic Museum** shares space in a converted chapel with a jewellery workshop. Linger in these lanes till dusk to experience the best of Mértola's dreamy atmosphere.

Alto (Upper) Alentejo

Évora, 145 kilometres (90 miles) southeast of Lisbon, is the Alentejo's pride and joy, a city of great age and beauty. Its most brilliant era was from the fourteenth to sixteenth centuries under the patronage of the House of Avis when it was favoured by royalty, artists and intellectuals. Tourists love the place (you should book accommodation) but so far the streets and *palácios* remain unharmed, making this one of the most enjoyable destinations in southern Portugal. In 1986 its inner walled town was declared part of the World Patrimony by UNESCO.

The highlight is the second-century **Temple of Diana**, one of the country's most evocative legacies of the Romans' 400-year occupation. The raised platform of Corinthian columns, topped with Estremoz marble capitals, was used as a fortress in the Middle Ages and later as a slaughterhouse. Opposite is the former **Monastery dos Lóios**, founded in the fifteenth century and now a government *pousada* (see Accommodation, page 176).

Access to the adjoining **Lóios church** dedicated to St John the Evangelist (the name Lóios comes from the order of Canons Regular, founded by St Eloi) can be tricky since the Cadaval family who own it keep erratic opening hours (try Sunday mornings). But it is worth perservering to see the early eighteenth-century *azulejos* (there are even *trompe l'oeil azulejo* windows). Downhill, in the **Palace of the Dukes of Cadaval**, an art gallery has sombre ecclesiastical portraits and a huge revolving seventeenth-century Gregorian music stand.

The best paintings in town are in the **Museu de Évora** (open 10 am–12.30 pm, 2–5 pm, closed Monday) and include sixteenth-century Flemish and Portuguese works (heavy-lidded saints by the famous Frei Carlos are distinctive) and a remarkable polyptych on the life of the Virgin, painted by Flemish artists in Portugal in the sixteenth century.There is an absorbing collection of stone carvings, particularly a fourteenth-century Annunciation in marble, the 1535 cenotaph of D Alvaro da Costa by the sympathetic Frenchman Chanterène, and a tiny Bacchante, headless and nearly 2,000 years old but still dancing merrily.

The adjacent thirteenth-century **Cathedral** (probably on the site of an earlier mosque) has a simple Gothic interior, with eye-catching bands of mortar around its granite pillars and rosary chains supporting huge chandeliers. The cloisters are lovely, with attractive stone-carved arches, and a good rooftop view of the town. In the **Treasury** are two particular gems: a tiny seventeenth-century bejewelled cross, and a thirteenth-century ivory Virgin, her belly generously opened to reveal intricately carved scenes of her life.

More mortar bands feature in the **Church of São Francisco**, unremarkable except for its ghoulish **Capela dos Ossos** (Chapel of Bones): the walls and columns are made from 5,000 monks' bones as a lesson in the mortality of man ('We bones here wait for your bones', says the entrance inscription). Dim orange lighting and a crumpled skeleton drooped on one wall add an extra tingle to the atmosphere.

The **Renaissance fountain** in the busy Largo da Porta da Moura and the pretty **Travessa da Caraca** are both worth seeking out, but the best discoveries are down by the sixteenth-century **aqueduct**; from the main Praça do Giraldo, follow Rua João de Deus until it becomes Rua José Elias Garcia and then turn right into any of the little *travessas* leading to the arches of the aqueduct.

A cosy village life huddles around here, with houses built beneath the arches opposite workshops, bars and grocery stores. Where the aqueduct joins the city wall, turn left into Rua Candido dos Reis to find the sixteenth-century **Convent of Calvário** (the door is to the right, in Travessa dos Lagares). Ring the bell, and a nun will lead you through rooms of polished furniture to cloisters full of flowers and chattering children (the convent now serves as an orphanage). The chapel has *azulejos* to the ceiling and a shower of gilt woodwork.

From Évora you have an excellent choice of day-trips, though **Estremoz**, 46 kilometres (28 miles) northeast, is so pleasant you may want to stay overnight, especially if you can time it for the huge Saturday market that specializes in local pottery. The spacious Rossio main square, dominated by a thirteenth-century castle on the hilltop above, gives this old town a deceptively grand aura. In fact, it has a village atmosphere—friendly, curious, and proud. The Rossio's Café Alentejano is the best place to people-watch.

The former palace of Dom Dinis within the castle walls is now one of the country's most impressive *pousadas* with baronial style furnishings and a grand stairway of *azulejos*. Climb right to the top of the **keep** for giddy views down the oil-pouring holes. The **Municipal Museum** opposite has a collection of the curious Estremoz pottery figures while upstairs are typical Alentejan rooms—all pretty painted furniture and fancy lacework.

But the best folk display is in the quaint, two-room **Rural Museum** (Rossio 62, open 10 am–1 pm, 3–6 pm, closed Monday) whose attendants lovingly point out every piece, from cowbells to cork calf protectors, knotted jugs to a huge olive press, and drinking bowls to socks and mittens.

Situated as it is in the heart of marble country, many of the streets in Estremoz gleam with unexpected grandeur (Rua dos Carvoeiros, downhill and right from the Turismo, is one of the most attractive) but the biggest surprises are in nearby **Vila Vicosa** and **Borba** where even the bus-stops are made of marble. Borba itself, surrounded by marble quarries, has little else to recommend it, but Vila Vicosa is dominated by the vast **Ducal Palace** (open 9 am–1 pm, 2–6 pm, closed Monday), seat of the Dukes of Bragança from the early sixteenth century until the fall of the monarchy in 1910 (the reluctant eighth Duke became king in 1640 after a popular revolt against Spanish rule).

The sumptuous interior soon grows tedious but attention picks up in the massive kitchens with their 600 copper pans and a room devoted to the spit. The bedrooms, too, bring the royal family into more intimate perspective, especially the assassinated King Carlos whose paintings and sketches fill many walls.

At the other end of town, the old walled citadel has a renovated **castle** (former residence of the dukes before the palace was built), crammed with stuffed animals and birds (even the chandeliers are made of antlers)—not a great place for animal-lovers.

Walled towns are a speciality of this borderland area, and none is more impressive than **Elvas**, just a dozen kilometres (7.5 miles) from Spain. One of the strongest fortresses in the country (and in Europe), its original Moorish castle was supplemented by seventeenth-century ramparts, gates, moats, bastions and forts. Circle the city by following the streets beneath the walls (about five kilometres or three miles) to see how Elvas resisted countless Spanish assaults.

Évoramonte is on a much smaller scale. On the edge of the Ossa range 17 kilometres (11 miles) southwest of Estremoz, its castle is visible for miles around, but the old walled village has long been forgotten: there are no shops, no bars, no schools, just a few old men and drowsy dogs languishing at the church. The cement renovations of the castle simply show how to ruin a good ruin, while the most famous house in town—where the 1834 Convention was signed, ending the civil war—is distinguished only by a simple plaque and slightly fancier lace curtains than its neighbours'.

By contrast, the tiny hilltop fortress of **Monsaraz** is as spectacular inside as from a distance. Fields of wild flowers, cork and olive trees provide a magical approach from Mourão, 12 kilometres (seven miles) south. Occupied in turn by Romans, Visigoths, Moors and Knights Templars, its castle dates from the thirteenth century, but in the main cobbled street are sixteenth-and seventeenth-century white-washed houses with wrought-iron balconies and coats of arms. Monsaraz used to feel remote; now tour-buses make regular calls, and there are cafés, souvenir shops, rooms to rent, and a **museum** of sacred art next to the church. Only the back-streets still have a wilder atmosphere, with crumbling cottages, cacti, and dreamy views through chinks in the wall to the floral Alentejan plains below.

But for the prettiest hilltop fortress, first place must go to **Marvão**, an unspoilt medieval village 800 metres (2,400 feet) high on a spur of the Serra de São Mamede range, 19 kilometres (11 miles) northeast of Portalegre. Even the *pousada* here is discreetly tucked amongst the narrow lanes where several white-washed houses feature Manueline windows and Gothic doorways—no. 1 Rua do Castelo is a striking example (if the door is open, take a peep at its hallway, decorated with old keys, scissors, stirrups and locks).

Tiny stone faces above doorways are another delight—one will greet you at the Casa do Povo in Rua de Cima. The **Municipal Museum** (open 9 am–12.30 pm, 2–5.30 pm) in the former Church of Santa Maria below the thirteenth-century castle includes a Roman skeleton, Alentejan costumes, and fascinating local medicinal herbs *(crendices)*. Go up on the castle ramparts for the view: Marvão seems literally to merge into jagged rock. Down the road is the **Monastery of NS da Estrêla** (now a Misericordia hospital); in its church a sweet elderly nun pats the altarpiece (and almost everything else) with loving pride, murmuring 'This is marble! And this! And this!'

The nearby spa town of **Castelo de Vide** is another hilltop gem, with surrounding wooded slopes that 'give to the climate,' says the local Turismo brochure, 'a restful sweetness and to the landscape paradisiacal perspective.' Indeed, the best perspective of the walled town is from the **Chapel Nossa Senhora da Penha** two kilometres south, on a pine-forested hilltop.

Castelo de Vide is a busy little place, keeping up with time (there are several hotels on the outskirts and a new housing area), but the old lanes wriggling below the castle still have a medieval aura. From the granite **Fonte de Vila**, where, at dusk, villagers bring their mules to drink, a lane of plump white-washed houses with Gothic doors and potted flowers leads into the **Judiaria**, one of the few original medieval Jewish quarters left in Portugal. The thirteenth-century **synagogue** displays its wooden tabernacle and a shelf for scriptures, cut into the stone wall. An even quieter world exists within the **castle** walls, where a **Turismo** office and craft centre are housed in the former prison.

Off the Track

If you are heading to or from the Algarve, there is an enticing route between Monchique and **Odemira**, a market town some 20 kilometres (12 miles) from the Atlantic. A Tuscan landscape of rolling hills and fields of wild flowers makes **Sta Clara-à-Velha** a memorable mid-way piece of paradise. On the coast, **Almograve** offers a wilder, rockier setting than nearby **Vila Nova de Milfontes**, which has become increasingly popular.

But for untamed atmosphere, the countryside around Évora is hard to beat. Scattered in the area are **stone tombs** and circles of the Megalithic culture which flourished in the upper Alentejo between 4000 and 2000 BC. A day's dolmen-hunting from Évora can take you to some extraordinary places: near **Valverde**, ten kilometres (six miles) southwest, is the dolmen of **Zambujeiro**, at five metres (17 feet) high the largest in Europe. It lies under a corrugated-iron shelter in a field of cork-oaks and flowers, flown over by herons and hawks. With luck you might stumble on even more remote stone mysteries. The Turismo pamphlet, 'Megalithic Itinerary' will put you vaguely in the right direction.

Lisbon

Like Rome, Lisbon is built on seven low hills, commanding a superb harbour at the estuary of the River Tagus. Its fine position first attracted Phoenician settlers (who called it Alis Ubbo, 'delightful shore') over 3,000 years ago, and it has been a prosperous port ever since. The Romans, followed by the Moors, had a strong foothold here, but in 1147 the Moors were driven out by Dom Afonso Henriques with the help of a ruffian bunch of passing crusaders. Afonso III first chose Lisbon as the capital in 1255.

Also like Rome, Lisbon has had more than its share of glory and tragedy: one moment the opulent seat of a vast empire, the world's most important trading centre, and the next a scene of devastation, reduced to rubble in 1755 by a tremendous earthquake, its power forever weakened. During its sixteenth-century heyday, Luís de Camões described Lisbon as 'princess of the world, before whom even the ocean bows'. But when the ocean rose up in the earthquake's tidal wave, only an ironic Voltaire thought to capture the moment in his famous philosophical work, *Candide*.

There is still a sense of unfinished tragedy about Lisbon. Perhaps this is due to the sad, soul-searing *fado* (see Music, page 45) laments that first seeped from the old Alfama district in the nineteenth century and continue to be the heart and soul of the city's nightlife entertainment. Or perhaps it is the faded glory of its old houses, trundling cable cars and shabby back streets. Or the dreamy *miradouros* (viewpoints), where Lisboans love to linger, gazing over the terracotta-tiled city towards the golden 'straw sea' Tagus. Indeed, this is not a place where you are going to feel rushed: atmosphere is all.

And it can be pleasantly experienced. The great thing about Lisbon is that it is a manageable city. Walking is the easiest and best way to explore its steep streets, with trams as an enjoyable back-up. Wide, tree-lined avenues, mosaic pavements and sidewalk cafés (including some art nouveau classics) provide plenty of pleasures en route. The streets and squares are full of life, teeming with lottery ticket-sellers, window-shoppers and shoeshiners, hawkers, artists and buskers. It is a cosmopolitan life, too, with many *retournados* from Portugal's former colonies such as Angola, the Cape Verde Islands and Mozambique adding a new zest to both business and entertainment.

Getting To and From

The **airport** is about 25 minutes away by taxi (roughly Es.800) or by bus no. 44 or 45 from Praça dos Restauradores. **Long-distance trains** (international and from the north) arrive at Santa Apolónia Station, east of Praça do Comércio. **Local trains** arrive at the central Rossio square station. From the south, trains stop at the suburb of Barreiro and connect with a ferry service to the Fluvial station, Praça do Comércio. The main **RN** (national company) **bus stations** are at Avenida Casal Ribeiro for destinations north and Praça de Espanha or 75 Avenida Cinco de Outubro for southern destinations.

Getting Around

Taxis are metered and cheap (although not always easily available at night). **City buses** go just about everywhere (routes are marked at bus-stops) and accept the same tickets as **trams** *(eléctricos)* which trundle up some of the city's steepest gradients (tram-stops are marked by *paragem* signs hanging from the cables). It is cheaper and easier to buy a block of tickets *(modulos*, Es.500 for ten) than to pay on board. These are available at various kiosks near major bus-stops, or more conveniently at the Elevador Santa Justa ticket booth which also sells **tourist passes** (Es.980 for four days, Es.1,355 for seven days, for all public transport) and provides Carris bus and tram maps. The limited **metro** is only really useful for getting to the Gulbenkian Museum. **Commuter ferries** across the Tagus to Cacilhas from Praça do Comércio or Cais do Sodré provide one of the best afternoon views of the city. Two-hour **river cruises** run between April and October from Praça do Comércio, at 3 pm or 10 pm. Carris operate two **Tourist Tramcar tours** from Praça do Comércio: 'Hills of Lisbon' at least three times daily from 7 May to 16 September; and 'Tagus Line' (to Belém) twice a day from 29 June to 31 August. Details and tickets from the **Turismo** office in Praça dos Restauradores (open Monday to Saturday 9 am–8 pm, 10 am–6 pm on Sundays).

Old Town: The Alfama and Castle

The **Alfama** is the oldest part of Lisbon, one of the few areas to have escaped the 1755 earthquake because of its steep stone foundations. Early morning is the time to be here, when buxom fisherwomen spread eels, squid and sardines onto wooden tables by their doorsteps, and yell out prices to passers-by. Despite encroaching commercialization (fancy tourist restaurants and extensive renovation work), this grass-roots corner of Lisbon still has the essence of a fishing village. The tangle of narrow lanes (called *becos*) are crammed with cheap workers' cafés and tiny grocery stores, bars for real drinkers and barbers' scruffy salons; there are even a couple of huge communal laundry yards (off Beco do Meixias and through the arch of Beco das Cruzes), and in every alley the sound of caged songbirds and flapping laundry.

The **cathedral** *(Sé)*, just west of the Alfama, has an impressive fortress appearance but inside is surprisingly dull. First built in the twelfth century and rebuilt after various earthquakes, it has a very simple Romanesque nave. More captivating is the fourteenth-century tomb of long-haired Lopo Fernandes Pacheco, with a very large dog at his feet. The **cloisters** seem half-forgotten—a collection of ruined arches, burnt columns and bits of abandoned stone.

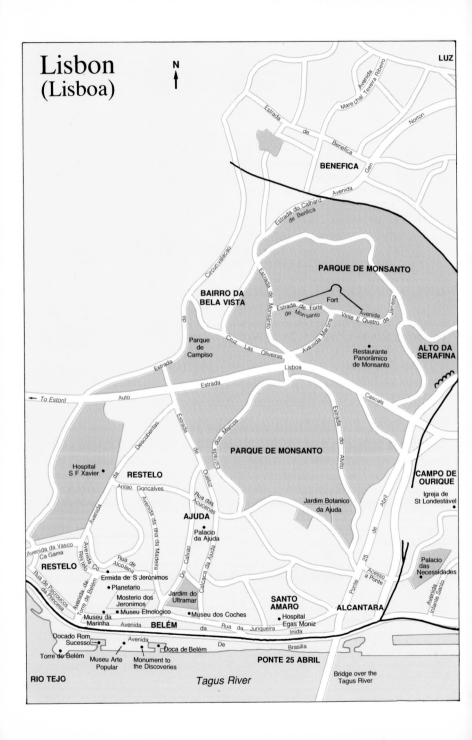

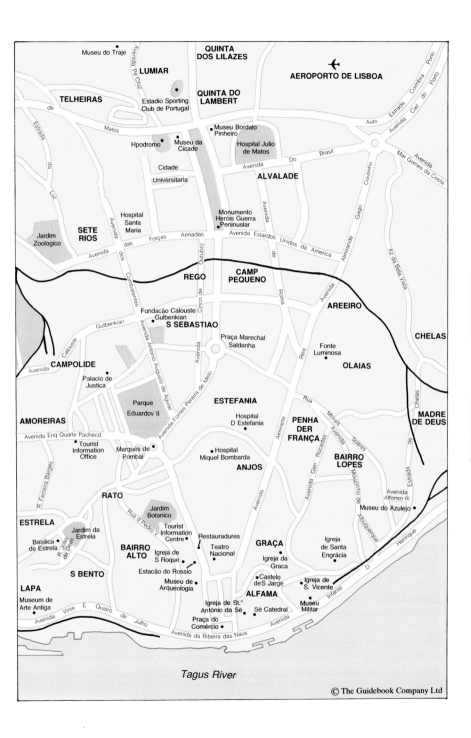

Museu do Traje

LUMIAR

QUINTA DOS LILAZES

AEROPORTO DE LISBOA

TELHEIRAS

Estadio Sporting
Club de Portugal

QUINTA DO
LAMBERT

Matos

Hpodromo

Museu da
Cicade

Museu Bordalo
Pinheiro

Hospital Julio
de Matos

Auto

Estrada

Coimbra

Porto

Criel

do

Porto

Avenida

Mar Gomes da Costa

Avenida

de

Cidade

Universitaria

Do

Brasil

ALVALADE

Coutinho

Estrada

da

Luz

Jardim
Zoologico

SETE
RIOS

Avenida

Hospital
Santa
Maria

Forças

Armadas

Monumento
Heróis Guerra
Peninuslar

Avenida Estardos

Unidos da America

Gago

Almirande

Az da Bela Vista

Avenida

dos

das

Combatentes

REGO

CAMP
PEQUENO

de

Outubro

Avenida

de

AREEIRO

CHELAS

Gulbenkian

Calouste

Fundacão Calouste
Gulbenkian

S SEBASTIAO

Cinco

de

Avenida

Praça Marechal
Saldanha

Roma

Reis

Fonte
Luminosa

Avenida

OLAIAS

CAMPOLIDE

Avenida

Palacio de
Justica

Avenida

Antonio

Augusto

de

Aguiar

Avenida

Avenida

Fontes

Pereira

de

Melo

ESTEFANIA

Rua

Chelas

AMOREIRAS

Avenida Enq Quarte Pachecd

Parque
Eduardov II

Hospital
D Estefania

Almirante

PENHA
DER
FRANÇA

Avenida

Gen

Rocadas

Morais

Soares

Avenida

MADRE
DE DEUS

de

R. Ferreira Barges

Tourist
Information
Office

Marquès de
Pombal

Hospital
Miquel Bombarda

ANJOS

BAIRRO
LOPES

Mouzinho

de

Estrada

RATO

Jardim
Botanico

Avenida
Alfonso III

Museu do Azulejo

ESTRELA

Rua

d

Pedro

Tourist
Information
Centre

Restauradures

GRAÇA

Igreja
de Santa
Engrácia

Albuquerque

Henrique

Basilica
de Estrela

Jardim da
Estrela

R

São

de

Deus

BAIRRO
ALTO

Igreja de
S Roque

Teatro
Nacional

Igreja da
Graca

S BENTO

Estacão do Rossio

Museu de
Arqueologia

Castelo
deS Jarge

ALFAMA

Igreja de
S. Vicente

D

LAPA

Museum de
Arte Antiga

Avenida

Vinte

E

Quatro

de

Julho

Igreja de St.°
António da Sé

Praça do
Comércio

Sé Catedral

Avenida

Museu
Militar

Infante

Avenida da Ribeira das Naus

Tagus River

© The Guidebook Company Ltd

Keep climbing to reach the **castle of São Jorge** (open 9 am–9 pm), the ancient heart of Lisbon's defences, now renovated into a chic leisure area, adorned with peacocks and ponds, aviaries of hoarse-throated ravens, and beret-hatted artists. The best thing about the place is the tremendous view of the city from the walls.

East of the castle (tram 28 from the Baixa), the **Church and Monastery of São Vicente de Fora** is a sombre place of grey stone, built by the Italian Filippo Terzi during the seventeenth-century period of Spanish rule. Off the cloister, featuring eighteenth-century *azulejos* (glazed tiles), the former refectory is now a mausoleum for the Bragança ruling family with rows of black marble tombs.

On Tuesday and Saturday mornings, the sounds of a **flea market** disturb the ghosts of the mausoleum from behind the church. The market mostly features cheap clothes and shoes and a familiar assortment of junk—bells and brassware, tin watering cans, discarded shower heads, and broken spectacles. If you shuffle around the shops at the side of the covered market you may find some useless little knick-knack you have always fancied.

The nearby **Church of Santa Engrácia** is hard to overlook with its huge dome: this was only finished in 1966 after work on the church—which started 284 years earlier—was thwarted by storms, lethargy and lack of interest. Now the National Pantheon, it contains gracious ochre and grey marble cenotaphs (including those of Prince Henry the Navigator and Luís de Camões). The guide takes you by lift to the rooftop for panoramic views and surreptitious sales of second-rate postcards.

Heart of the City: The Baixa

After the Great Earthquake of 1755, the autocratic future Marquis of Pombal initiated a revolutionary new plan for the city: a grid of straight, wide streets for each trade stretching from the riverside Praça do Comércio to the Rossio. The **Baixa** (lower town) still stands out for its rigid simplicity, although the pedestrianization of Rua Augusta (once the reserve of cloth-dealers) has brought a touch of very unPombal-like anarchy into the area, which already has a fair share of meandering hawkers.

Everything and everyone tends to gravitate towards the Baixa: the Rossio and Praça do Comércio are transport hubs (the latter is even used as a car park, dominated by the equestrian statue of Dom José) and most major offices are located here. There are still plenty of shops according to Pombal's plan—silversmiths in Rua da Prata, goldsmiths in Rua do Ouro (renamed Rua Aurea)—but the most fashionable area for shoppers is now in nearby **Chiado** (the elegant old **Brasileira café** at 120 Rua Garrett is *the* place to take refreshment, among a traditional clientele of intellectuals). As usual in Lisbon, there is a novel way to get to Chiado—by the turn-of-the-century iron **Elevador de Santa Justa** (often attributed to Eiffel but actually designed by a man called Mesnier) which deposits you high above the Baixa near the Largo do Carmo.

High Town, Low Life: Bairro Alto

One of Lisbon's most fascinating older quarters, the Bohemian Bairro Alto comes alive at night, when the narrow sixteenth-century streets reveal a carnival of *fado* houses, trendy bars and restaurants. Getting up here provides an excuse to use the **funicular trams** of Elevador da Gloria (from next to the Turismo in Praça dos Restauradores), Elevador da BICA (from Rua de São Paulo), or the Elevador de Santa Justa (from Rua do Ouro).

Almost on the doorstep of the Elevador de Santa Justa is the Convento do Carmo, transformed into a stunning Gothic ruin by the 1755 earthquake and now housing a moderately interesting **Archaeological Museum** (open 10 am–1 pm, 2–5 pm, closed Monday) with various Visigothic and Luso-Romano remains and a glass case of gruesome Peruvian mummies.

The artistic highlight of the area is the late sixteenth-century **Church of São Roque**—not that it is apparent from the plain façade. But step inside and a custodian will proudly escort you from one richly adorned side chapel to the next, leaving the best to last: the **Chapel of São João Baptista** (fourth on left), resplendently furnished with angels of Carrara marble, columns of lapis lazuli, altar of amethyst, walls of mosaic and layers of gold, silver and bronze. Originally constructed in Rome in 1742, the chapel was blessed by the Pope, dismantled and shipped to Lisbon in three boats. It is best seen with the organ playing at full blast (try late morning).

Resuscitation is close at hand: the **Solar do Vinho do Porto** (Port Wine Institute) at 45 Rua de São Pedro de Alcântara is a cool and snobbish bar where you can savour up to several hundred varieties of port.

Museums

The number one sight in Lisbon is the **Calouste Gulbenkian Museum** (Avenida de Berna, open 1 June–30 September: Tuesday, Thursday, Friday, Sunday, 10 am–5 pm; Wednesday, Saturday, 2–7.30 pm; rest of year: 10 am–5 pm, closed Mondays). This modern, purpose-built complex houses the collection of art that the Armenian oil magnate bequeathed to Portugal (where he lived for 13 years until his death in 1955). The Gulbenkian Foundation funds a host of other artistic and cultural activities (pick up a leaflet here for details) and sells some of the best and cheapest art postcards in town in the museum lobby.

Gulbenkian chose only the very best. The result is a collection of manageable size, in which every piece is a gem. Even coins suddenly look interesting. Detailed notes (sold at the entrance) are worth picking up since the showcases are modest with information. The museum is divided into two parts—Oriental and Classical, and European—and each is worth a separate visit.

In the first section, the Egyptian Room is outstanding, covering almost every period from 2700 BC to the first century. Prize items include a beautifully simple alabaster bowl, the finely-chiselled faces of King Amenophis III and Judge Bes and a series of bronze cats (their ears pierced for earrings). Note, too,

an extraordinarily modern-looking Head of a Priest carved from green schist (no. 35). But it is the Islamic display that has the most surprises, including sensuously-shaped mosque lamps from the fourteenth century and sixteenth-century Turkish faience of bright greens and blues.

Look for your favourite European painter in the European section and chances are you will find him: just about everyone is represented. My favourites included a serene Annunciation (no. 895) by Dierick Bouts, and *The Baptism of Christ* by Francesco Francia. Ghirlandaio's famous *Portrait of a Young Woman* is quite startling face-to-face. Masterpieces by Rubens and Rembrandt (especially Rembrandt's haunting *Figure of an Old Man*, no. 967) are among the best representations of the seventeenth century. The eighteenth-century section has works by all the big names: keep an eye out for de la Tour's *Portrait of Duval de l'Épinoy,* (no. 913) which is one of the art world's best portraits of vain nobility. After fussy Louis XV and XVI furniture, Aubusson tapestries and Spanish ceramics, the art nouveau jewellery by René Lalique (in a separate room downstairs) makes a refreshing finale.

Across the gardens is the new **Gulbenkian Museum of Modern Art** with exclusively Portuguese works, notably by Amadeo de Souza Cardoso and Almada Negreiros. If you are prepared to queue, the café serves delicious salads.

The **Museu Nacional de Arte Antiga** (Rua das Janelas Verdas, open 10 am–1 pm, 2.30–5 pm, closed Monday) concentrates on Portuguese art from the eleventh to nineteenth centuries, early European paintings and eighteenth-century French silverware. But the highlight is the famous polyptych of the *Adoration of St Vincent* painted in 1467–70 by Nuno Gonçalves, one of the few early Portuguese painters who resisted the strong Flemish influence of the time, although he may well have learnt some of their techniques. Among the tapestry of figures paying homage to St Vincent—from kings and queens to knights and beggars—spot the leading light of this Age of Discoveries: Prince Henry the Navigator (in the left central panel, with the floppy hat).

Other notable works are a luminous *Annunciation* by Frei Carlos and, in striking contrast, the horrific *Temptations of St Anthony* by Hieronymous Bosch, with its flying fish, man-sized rats, and skeleton harp-players. Works by Dürer, Della Robia and Rodin restore the harmony. The museum's new wing shows the artistic influence of Portugal's overseas explorations: the most striking results are Japanese painted screens, with big-nosed Portuguese traders and Jesuit priests, which were inspired by the arrival of the Portuguese in Japan's Tanegaxima island in 1543.

The **Museu da Cidade**, City Museum (245 Campo Grande, open 10 am–1 pm, 2–6 pm, closed Monday), housed in an old palace, shows you what Lisbon was like before and after the 1755 earthquake with a multitude of old maps, prints, *azulejos* and even a vast scale model. The nineteenth-century costume books and prints of Lisbon lifestyles are very revealing.

The **Museu do Azulejo**, Tile Museum (Madré de Deus Convent, open 10 am–5 pm, closed Monday) provides a comprehensive survey of how this art form developed from the fourteenth century to the present day, with samples displayed around the sunny cloisters of the convent and in a modern extension. The vast pre-earthquake *azulejo* panorama of Lisbon tends to grab all the attention, but other gems are a seventeenth-century hairy Bacchus with grapes at his groin, and a delightful sixteenth-century *Shepherds' Adoration*.

Even if you are not an a*zulejos* fan, the **Madré de Deus church** itself is well worth a visit. Eighteenth-century Dutch tiles cover the lower walls of the ornately gilt nave, with paintings above on the life of St Francis. The chapter house is one of the richest in town, with a coffered gilt ceiling framing sixteenth-and seventeenth-century paintings and yet more walls of azulejos. It is completely over the top; the last thing you would be able to do here is keep your mind on prayers.

The **Museu da Marioneta**, Puppet Museum (13 Largo Rodrigues de Freitas, open 11 am–1 pm, 3–6 pm, closed Monday) is a tiny den crammed with puppet curiosities including Asian exhibits and nineteenth-century Portuguese figures; pity there are no English captions, but kids love it nonetheless.

Around Lisbon

Belém (20 minutes by tram 15, 16 or 17 westwards from Praça do Comércio) is the historical heart and soul of the nation. It was from here, on 8 July 1497, that Vasco da Gama set sail on his voyage to discover the sea route to India, launching Portugal into its Golden Age.

The **Jerónimos Monastery** (open 10 am–5 pm, until 6.30 pm in summer, closed Monday), built by Dom Manuel to thank the Virgin for da Gama's success, epitomizes that age in a brilliant outburst of Manueline confidence and originality. Work began in 1502 (with funds from a tax on the spices from the newly discovered lands), largely directed by Diogo de Boitac following Gothic lines and, later, by the Spaniard João de Castilho who had more Renaissance ideas. The result is an ingenious balance of styles evident throughout the monastery.

The south doorway in the vast façade places Prince Henry the Navigator above a sea of figures and pinnacles, but the entrance to the church is through Chanterène's west doorway, now hardly noticeable under a modern cover. Inside, you become immediately aware of a sense of spaciousness—the artistic equivalent of days at sea—contrasting with a mass of Manueline decoration. The vaulting over both nave and aisles resisted the 1755 earthquake but the stained glass windows are copies of the shattered originals. Appropriately, the tombs of Vasco da Gama and Luís de Camões lie near each other, in the lower chancel. Most striking of all is the two-tiered **cloister**: a mass of carved stone coils, cables, canopies, and double arches.

The **Museu da Marinha** (open 10 am–midday, 2–5 pm, closed Monday) is housed in the monastery's west wing. Sailors will love its ship models (the early *caravelas* are best), old globes and the cabin of the turn-of-the-century royal Yacht Amelia, complete with pianola and fireplace. The annexe of *galeotas* (barges) is dull, and not even the huge eighteenth-century Royal Barge with model oarsmen (some missing) generates much excitement. The **Museu Nacional de Arqueologia e Etnologia** (open same hours as above) in the east wing is full of schoolchildren taking notes on prehistoric flints, skeletons and dolmens; if you can get past them, the Roman jewellery section is worth a visit for its stylish gold bangles, rings and necklaces.

The **Torre de Belém**, Belém Tower (open 10 am–5 pm, until 6.30 pm in summer) is a short walk from the monastery. It no longer commands the middle of the Tagus but is still lapped by the river's receding waters. Built in the final years of Dom Manuel's reign (1515–20) it has become the most popular symbol of the Age of Discoveries, with that era's two dominant motifs: the armillary sphere (representing the globe) and the cross of the Order of Christ (emblazoned in red on all the discoverers' ships). With its Moorish-inspired turrets, sentry boxes, battlements and balconies, it is an intricate little Manueline masterpiece, full of grace and power.

The view from the Tower is eclipsed by that from the **Monument to the Discoveries** (open 9 am–7 pm), opposite the monastery. Built in 1960 to commemmorate the 500th anniversary of the death of Prince Henry, its stylized prow is carved with heroes from the period. Inside are exhibitions on, of course, the Age of Discoveries.

The adjacent **Museu de Arte Popular** (open 10 am–12.30 pm, 2–5 pm, closed Monday) in a badly-signposted riverside warehouse provides an over-view of Portugal's folk arts, region by region, with everything from bagpipes and spiked dog collars to saddles, straw coats, and painted fishing prows. It is well presented, if rather lacking in atmosphere.

The **Museu de Coches**, Coach Museum (Praça Afonso de Abuquerque, east of the monastery, open 10 am–1 pm, 2.30–5.30 pm, until 6.30 pm in summer, closed Monday) is one of those places tourists are told they must see. Boasting the world's finest collection, it certainly has a few impressive eighteenth-century royal vehicles, gilded and painted like a baroque chapel, but the poorly-captioned exhibits quickly pall.

The **Museu de Etnologia** (Avenida Ilha da Madeira, uphill beside the monastery, open 10 am–12.30 pm, 2–5 pm, closed Monday) makes a refreshing change from Belém's emphasis on the fifteenth century. Its ambitious, changing exhibitions complemented by music and slides can keep you absorbed for hours.

Linked to Lisbon by train and a notoriously dangerous highway, the **Estoril coast** has long been a favourite haunt of Lisboans. **Estoril** itself, 26 kilometres

A Grand Procession

*I*could hardly sleep for the jingling of bells, beating of drums and flourishings of trumpets which struck up at daybreak in honour of that pompous festival the Corpo de Deos. I had half a mind to have stayed at home writing to you and reading Camoens; but I was told such wonders of the procession in honour of this glorious day that I could not refuse giving myself a little trouble in order to witness them. The streets in the quarter of Lisbon I inhabit, as well as those through which I passed in my way to the Patriarchal, were entirely deserted. A pestilence seemed to have swept the Great Square and the busy environs of the India House and Exchange, for even vagrants, scavengers and beggars in the last stage of lousiness and decrepitude had all hobbled away to the scene of action. A few miserable curs sniffing at offals alone remained in the vacant streets, and a few palsied old women and a half dozen scabby children blubbering at being kept at home were the sole objects I could discover in the endless windows.*

I heard the murmur of the crowds assembled around the Patriarchal before I discovered them. We advanced with some difficulty between rows of soldiers drawn up in battle array, and upon turning a dark angle shaded by the high buildings of the Seminary adjoining the Patriarchal, discovered houses, shops and places all metamorphosed into tents, and hung from top to bottom with red damask, tapestry of a thousand colours, satin coverlids and fringed counterpanes glittering with gold. I thought myself in the midst of the Mogul's encampment. The front of the great church was magnificently curtained. It rises from a vast flight of steps, which being covered today with the Yeomen of the Queen's Guard in their rich parti-coloured velvet dresses and a multitude of priests bearing crosses and banners, formed one of the most theatrical perspectives I ever beheld. Flocks of sallow monks, white, brown and black, kept moving about continually like turkeys driving to market. This part of the procession lasting a tiresome while, I grew weary, left the balcony where we were most advantageously placed right opposite the great portal, and got into the church, where Mass was performing in full glory, incense ascending in clouds, thousands kneeling, and the light of innumerable tapers blazing on the diamonds and rubies of the ostensory elevated by the Patriarch with trembling devout hands to receive the mysterious wafer.

Before the close of the ceremony I regained my window to have a full view of the coming forth of the Sacrament. All was expectation and silence in the people. The Guards had ranged them on each side of the steps before the entrance of the church. At length a shower of aromatic herbs and flowers announced the approach of the Patriarch bearing the Host under a regal canopy surrounded by grandees and preceded by vast numbers of saintly mitred figures, their hands joined in prayer, their scarlet vestments sweeping the ground, their attendants bearing croziers, silver reliquaries and other insignia of pontifical grandeur. The procession, slowly descending the flights of stairs to the sound of choirs and the distant thunder of artillery, lost itself in a winding street decorated with splendid hangings, and left me with my senses in a whirl and my eyes dazzled like those of a saint just wakened from a vision of celestial splendour. My head swims at this moment and my ears tingle with a vibration of sounds — bells, voices, and the echoes of cannon prolonged by mountains and wafted over waters.

William Beckford, Portuguese Journal, 1787

(16 miles) west, is a snobbish resort where exiled royalty and the upper crust hide away in palatial villas, gamble at the casino or play golf at the Estoril Golf Club. **Cascais**, a few kilometres further west, is less snooty, and with less polluted beaches. The British will feel at home: there are scones for tea, the John Bull pub and Marks & Spencer in the high street.

If you make it to **Cabo da Roca**, 16 kilometres (ten miles) west of Sintra, you can buy a certificate (Es.250 or 400) to prove you have been at the westernmost point of Europe. There is actually nothing much to see, except the sea. But some nine kilometres (five miles) south is the pick of the area's beaches: **Guincho**, a surprisingly wild spot, with only a couple of hotels, and unpolluted (though strong) seas. Nearby **Colares**, en route to Sintra, is a wonderful place to get lost; follow the village's narrow lanes, covered by Moorish arches, until you reach the top of the ridge with its lush views of the surrounding Serra de Sintra range.

Five kilometres (three miles) northwest of Lisbon (20 minutes by train from Rossio), the blancmange-pink **Palace of Queluz** (open 10 am–1 pm, 2–5 pm, closed Tuesday) is like a miniature Versailles, all rococo elegance and fancy. Converted in the late eighteenth century from a hunting lodge to a summer retreat for Prince Dom Pedro (whose niece and wife, Maria I, spent her last mad years here), it became the royal family's permanent residence in 1794. Apart from the sumptuous Throne Room (which may be closed when visiting heads of state are staying in that wing), some fine Arraiolos carpets and inlaid wooden floors, the interior furnishings are surprisingly dull. Much more fun are the gardens with their clipped box trees, statues and fountains. There is even a canal basin adorned with a*zulejos* where the royal family went boating.

The town of **Mafra** (39 kilometres or 24 miles northwest of Lisbon) is completely dominated by its vast **Palace and Monastery** (open 10 am–1 pm, 2–5 pm, closed Tuesday). It was built by the extravagant Dom João V to honour a vow made when he prayed for an heir. In 1717, six years after the birth of his daughter, the first stone was laid.

It is the scale of the place that is stunning, rather than any architectural or interior details. With over 5,200 doorways, 2,500 windows and 45,000 labourers at work on its construction, it not surprisingly cost a fortune in Brazilian gold and drained the coffers dry. In the end it was not even very popular as a palace. But it did house a famous school of sculpture, inspired by the German architects and Italian artists on site for the construction. And it has since been very useful to the military: Wellington billeted his troops here and a military academy now occupies 85 percent of the place (you may hear their brass bands practising) with the police and town hall occupying another corner. Astonishing though it may seem, you will cover only ten percent of the premises on the lengthy tour.

The marble basilica is the centrepiece in the vast façade, flanked by Germanic-style wings and featuring Carrara marble statues in the porch. Pale pink-grey marble gives the interior an unexpected lightness; floor and ceiling designs match. Behind the church is the monastery, including a pharmacy, kitchen, and cells for 280 monks (including quarantine cells for the sick or insane).

Upstairs are the royal apartments off corridors 230 metres (700 feet) long. Most of the furniture was whisked away with the royal family to Brazil at the time of the French invasion, but there are still a few eye-catching pieces, including eighteenth-century pinball machines in the games room and hunting chairs of fur and deerskin made by prisoners for King Carlos. The library is fantastic: a bright baroque gallery of 40,000 books. It was supposed to have had a gilt ceiling to reflect in the mirrored walls but at this point, unfortunately, the money finally ran out. Cool, verdant **Sintra**, 28 kilometres (17 miles) northwest of Lisbon (45 minutes by train from Rossio) has an allure that few visitors have been able to resist—Romans, Moors or the British. For 500 years the Kings of Portugal chose Sintra as their summer resort, the nobility tucked villas and palaces amongst its lush hillsides and poets were enraptured by its natural beauty. Even Byron (who had few nice things to say about Portugal) managed to be charmed: 'Lo! Cintra's glorious Eden intervenes, in variegated maze of mount and glen', he wrote in *Childe Harold*. In a letter to his mother, he described the village of Cintra as 'perhaps the most delightful in Europe. . . It unites in itself all the wildness of the Western Highlands with the verdure of the south of France'.

It was a risky guess, seeing as he had never been to either place, but a good one: despite thousands of tourists daily, Sintra still has a wild aura. And its verdure is as enveloping as ever. Walking is the only way to really appreciate it but there are alternatives: **coach tours** with **Turismo** (below the National Palace) daily at 2 pm (except Monday); **taxis**, which have set rates for main places of interest (e.g. Es.1,500 for a one-hour return trip to Pena Palace); or, the most romantic, **horse and carriage** rides (Es.5,500 for return trip to Pena).

The **National Palace** (open 10 am–1 pm, 2–5 pm, closed Wednesday) dominates the old town with its two huge conical chimneys. João I built the main part of the palace at the end of the fourteenth century but later additions have created a confusion of styles. Visits are often tediously slow because of hordes of group tours. The really outstanding rooms, after the kitchens with their vast chimneys, only come at the end: the **Sala das Armas** with its coffered dome ceiling painted with the coats of arms of 72 noble families; the grand **Swan Room** (still used for important functions); and the delightful **Magpie Room**, its ceiling of magpies each clasping a rose with the words *Por bem* ('all in honour') supposedly referring to the reply of João I when caught kissing a lady-in-waiting. To mock court gossip, so the story goes, he had the ceiling painted with as many magpies as there were ladies-in-waiting.

The **Moorish Castle** is best approached by foot from town (Turismo have maps). At the end of a steep 50-minute walk you are rewarded with magnificent

Lisbon's ostentatious Praça do Comércio (top left); a city tram (top right);
the Lisbon panorama from the Castle of São Jorge (below)

A residential district in Belém

views of Sintra, Pena Palace and, on a clear day, even the sea at Cabo da Roca. Immediately below are fairytale *quintas* (country villas) and private palaces, such as the Chalé Biester (built in 1873) with its turquoise-ridged towers, and the 1904 pseudo-Manueline Quinta da Regaleira (known locally as 'Milhoes' because it cost millions to build), now owned by the Japanese millionaire Jorge Nichimura.

The energetic can take the turning below the castle and go on another 30 minutes' walk up to **Pena Palace** (open 10 am–5 pm, closed Monday) through its park of firs, camellias, redwoods and cypresses, ponds and fortress-follies.

Pena Palace appears above the trees like some whimsical Disneyland: all domes and towers and mock-Manueline gateways. It was built in 1840 by Dom Ferdinand II (whose Saxe Coburg-Gotha connections may explain Pena's similarity with Bavarian mock-medieval castles). In contrast with the National Palace, visitors are cossetted here: extensive, multi-lingual notes are in each room, and there is a musical accompaniment of Bach, Beethoven and Chopin (favourites of Dom Manuel II, the last royal to live here before the fall of the monarchy in 1910). Everything has been left in place from that moment, which creates an atmosphere as odd as the place itself.

The chapel of a sixteenth-century monastery is the only old part and features an alabaster altar by Chanterène. Elsewhere, the palace is a wonderfully crazy assortment: mahogany toilets made at the factory 'Hygienic', and bearded Turk statues holding candelabras; neo-Gothic ottomans and Masonic stained glass windows; a breakfast room in Meissen porcelain; and King Carlos' private study, its walls covered with his naughty sketches of gambolling naked women in the woods of Pena.

A couple of kilometres out of Sintra along the Colares road you reach the **Quinta de Monserrate,** famous for its beautiful and exotic gardens. After years of neglect these are now being restored, although the *quinta* itself remains closed. For some years at the end of the eighteenth century the eccentric English homosexual author, William Beckford (who fled England in the wake of a scandal) lived at Monserrate, importing a flock of sheep from Fonthill to enhance the landscape.

The **Convento dos Capuchos** (open 9 am–noon, 2–5 pm) is one of the most curious places in Sintra. Hidden in the depths of the forest six kilometres (four miles) west of Pena, the tiny sixteenth-century hermitage crouches among rocks and trees, with cork-lined cells for a dozen monks. One cell has the luxury of a cupboard, another some tiles in a niche. The chatty, perceptive custodian seems strangely at home here.

The Centre

Estremadura and Ribatejo

The Atlantic-hugging Estremadura province was the southernmost area wrested from the Moors in the thirteenth century (*estrema Durii* means 'farthest from the Douro'), the toe of Portugal's hold on Christianity. Now it could not be more central, or more important, containing not only Lisbon but also the country's most impressive Christian monuments—the Jerónimos Monastery, Mafra Monastery Palace, and Batalha and Alcobaça abbeys. There are some tremendous sweeps of countryside, too, such as from Mafra to Torres Vedras, with the sea on one side and rolling hills of farmland dotted with windmills on the other. To the south, the rocky and floral **Serra da Arrabida** is still surprisingly wild, though the beaches below quickly get crowded with Lisboans in summer.

Neighbouring Ribatejo pales by comparison. The romantic castle of Almourol and the Knights Templars' Convento de Cristo at Tomar are well worth seeing. But that's about it—unless you are a bullfighting fan: the flat land beside the Tagus (*ribatejo* means 'Tagus riverbank') is famous bull-breeding country. From July to September there are dozens of small festivals and **bullfights** in the region, kicked off by the Pamplona-style running of the bulls in Vila Franca de Xira the first two Sundays in July.

Alcobaça and Around

The **Cistercian Abbey of Alcobaça** is the grandest in the land. It was founded in 1178 by Dom Afonso Henriques, and became incredibly rich through its vast estates. It is said to have housed 999 monks in its heyday; their agricultural expertise helped create one of the most fertile areas in the region, and their grapevines are still among the best in the country. But the monks enjoyed life, too: even as late as the 1790s, when the eccentric English writer William Beckford came to visit, they indulged in an extravagant lifestyle, with 'perpetual gormandising. . . the fat waddling monks and sleek friars with wanton eyes, twanging away on the Jew's harp.' It all came to an abrupt end with the dissolution of religious orders in 1834.

The beautifully simple Gothic interior of Alcobaça's **church** makes a refreshing change from the complicated baroque and Manueline styles. Its richest treasures face each other in opposite transepts—the fourteenth-century tombs of Dom Pedro and Dona Inês de Castro, their detailed carving as dramatic as the story of their love. Pedro, son of Afonso V, fell in love with and secretly married Inês, the Spanish lady-in-waiting of his late wife. But believing Inês' family to be a threat, Dom Afonso had her murdered in 1355. Two years later, when Dom Pedro took the throne, he exhumed Inês' body and forced the court to do homage to his dead 'queen' by kissing her decomposed hand.

Henry the Navigator and the Age of Discoveries

Enough for us that the hidden half of the globe is brought to light, and the Portuguese daily go farther and farther beyond the equator. Thus shores unknown will soon become accessible; for one in emulation of another sets forth in labours and mighty perils.

(Peter Martyr, 1493)

Prince Henry was born at just the right time. The third son of King João I and his English queen Philippa first saw the light of an aquatic Oporto day in 1394, when Portugal's crusading zeal was beginning to mingle with an unprecedented spirit of adventure.

With a hostile Spain at its back, and with a new confidence gained from its victory against Spain at the 1386 Battle of Aljubarrota, this westernmost corner of

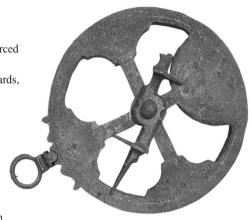

the Iberian peninsula was forced to look forward in the one direction open to it—westwards, across the unknown seas.

Motives for exploration were at first quite mixed: to fight the infidel Moors on their own land, to find the legendary Christian kingdom of Prester John (believed to rule a country in Africa beyond the Moorish

Infante D. Henrique
MCDIX   MCMLX

territories), and last but certainly not least, to acquire gold and slaves and reach the rich spice lands of the East. All this was part and parcel of the initial Portuguese thrust into the northern shores of Africa. But it was one man—Prince Henry—who was able to draw the strands together to direct it into becoming a national enterprise of discovery.

'This prince,' reported the contemporary chronicler Gomes Eanes de Zurara, 'was bound to engage in great and noble conquests, and above all he was bound to attempt the discovery of things which were hidden from other men, and secret.'

Fate set him on his course at an early age: when he was only 19 he was put in charge of building a fleet in Oporto to join the Crusade against Ceuta, the Muslim stronghold and trading centre on the north African coast. In July 1415, with his father and two brothers, he sailed out with a fleet of 200 ships. The armada won a decisive victory at Ceuta, but it was the loot found afterwards that made a greater impression on the serious young Prince Henry: in addition to the usual riches, there were hordes of exotic spices, gold, silver and silk that had arrived by caravans from the east. How could the Portuguese reach their source?

Prince Henry had always been the most studious of João's sons. An ascetic, rather unapproachable character, he lived like a monk and reputedly died a virgin. After Ceuta, he took himself away from the frivolities of court life and headed for Sagres and nearby Cape St Vincent. It was the bleakest, westernmost point on the southern Algarve coast, shaped like a ship, reported the geographer Strabo, 'where the land ends,' wrote Luís de Camões, 'and the sea begins.'

Here the Prince established a school of navigation, using his position as Governor of the Order of Christ (previously the crusading outfit called the Knights Templar) to fund research and exploration into the sea route from Europe to India. He surrounded himself with highly qualified astronomers and geographers, cartographers and seamen, boat-builders, travelling Jews, Arabs and astrologists—a think-tank of unprecedented scale and ambition.

Although the Prince is popularly known as 'the Navigator', he himself never went further than Tangier. He devoted his energies to his school and his mariners, and the overseas trade they established. The school improved navigation instruments and the art of cartography and taught mariners to use the stars to chart their positions, but undoubtedly its most important achievement was the redesign of the caravel to enable it to sail against the wind—the first European-built vessel able to do so and return home.

Considered to be one of the most efficient sailing ships ever designed, the *caravel* combined the Eastern-style triangular sail with the Western-style wide hull. It had some of the features of the Arab cargo-carrying *caravos* as well as the speed and manoeuvrability of the River Douro *caravelas*. With such a ship, the explorers felt a good deal more confident of approaching (and retreating from) the edge of the world—popularly believed to exist at Cape Bojador, on the west coast of Africa—and heading ever further into the unknown.

The navigators' first major discoveries were Madeira in 1419 and the Azores in 1427, both of which were subsequently colonized (they are still part of Portugal). But it was the African coast that held the Prince's attention. Between 1424 and 1434, he sent 15 expeditions to conquer the dreaded Cape Bojador. They all returned, defeated by fear, wrote Zurara. 'For, said the mariners, this much is clear, that beyond the Cape there is no race of men nor place of inhabitants. . .the currents are so terrible that no ship having once passed the Cape, will ever be able to return. . .these mariners of ours (were) threatened not only by fear but by its shadow. . .'

Finally, in 1434, Gil Eanes broke the boundary by steering far to the west as he approached the Cape, and south again when the Cape had been passed. 'Although the matter was a small one in itself,' wrote Zurara, 'yet on account of its daring it was reckoned great.' Indeed, it was a major watershed. From now on, the way beyond was open.

Although Prince Henry initiated a new colonial enterprise by setting up trading posts at each new landing place (incidentally always insisting that samples of fruits, nuts and plants were brought back, which led to some fascinating innovations in Portuguese cuisine), commercial rewards were at first very slim. Only in 1444 did Eanes return from Cape Blanco with the first human cargo—200 African slaves to be sold in Lagos. From then on, trade prospered, and dozens of caravels a year headed for the west African coast.

By the time Prince Henry died in Sagres in 1460, his mariners had reached Cape Verde, Guinea and Sierra Leone. There was no turning back. In 1482, Diogo Cau reached the mouth of the Congo River. Five years later, driven south by a storm, Bartolomeu Dias rounded the Cape of Good Hope.

Finally, in July 1497, Vasco da Gama set out with a fleet of four vessels for India. Eleven months later, he landed at Calicut. 'You owe great thanks to God, for having brought you to a country holding such riches!' he was told on arrival. Thanks also to Prince Henry, the Age of Discoveries briefly made Portugal a tremendous colonial power and irrevocably changed the course of history.

The huge emptiness of the monastic quarters only serves to emphasize their former grandeur. The **refectory** is as impressive as any church, with its vaulted ceiling and arcaded pulpit to one side (readings from the Bible accompanied the monks' banquets). The adjacent eighteenth-century **kitchens** are monumental, and include a channel of fresh water direct from the River Alcoa to provide a constant source of fresh fish. Beckford was led here by the Grand Priors, 'hand in hand, all three together. 'To the *kitchen*', said they in unison, 'to the kitchen'and that immediately'. In this 'most distinguished temple of gluttony in all Europe', he found mounds of fish and meat and 'pastry in vast abundance which a numerous tribe of lay brothers and their attendants were rolling out and puffing up into a hundred different shapes, singing all the while as blithely as larks in a corn field.'

The Cloister of Silence, dating from 1308, is a more modest affair, with delicately carved stone windows and a Manueline-style upper storey added in the sixteenth century. From the vast Gothic **dormitory** you can glimpse an unkempt courtyard where inmates of a mental asylum sadly wander. Many more corners of the Abbey are closed to the public. The best appreciation of the extent of the place is from the castle ruins, above the town, where locals walk their dogs among the poppies.

Just 20 kilometres (12 miles) north of Alcobaça, the **Abbey of Batalha** (open 9 am–5 pm) rises from the green valley below the main road like an apparition: all golden spires, towers, pinnacles, and flying buttresses. An exuberant masterpiece of Portuguese Gothic and Manueline architecture (in the same vein as the Jerónimos Monastery at Belém), it symbolizes the birth of Portuguese independence, won at the nearby Battle of Aljubarrota in 1385. Dom João of Aviz built the abbey after his victory against the far superior forces of Juan I of Castile, his rival to the throne.

Even from afar you feel dwarfed by the monument's towering proportions. The interior Gothic nave is just as tremendous—tall, plain bays, warmed by modern stained glass windows. To the right, the **Capela do Fundador** (Founder's Chapel) is the icing on the cake; an octagonal lantern topped by an elaborate star vault honours the central tombs of Dom João I and his English wife, Philippa of Lancaster. Their effigies lie hand in hand, a symbol of the closeness of the English-Portuguese alliance. Tombs of their four younger sons (including the one of Prince Henry the Navigator) rest against the south wall.

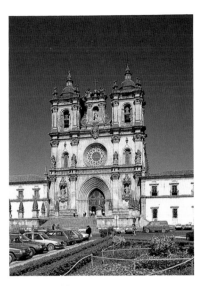

The English connection shows in hints of English Perpendicular style throughout Batalha, but the **Claustro Real** (Royal Cloister) is pure Portuguese, the original Gothic design embellished by later Manueline flourishes—columns of coils and pearls, and a masterful rendering in stone of branches, fruit and vegetables.

The stomping of soldiers' feet echo through the cloisters when the guard changes at the Tomb of the Unknown Soldiers in the **Chapter House**, remarkable for its unsupported vault, 19 metres (58 feet) square. An incongruous military museum is housed in the refectory, but note the superb fountain Lavabo opposite, an intricately carved corner of the cloisters, coiling the sun's rays among its tracery.

Beyond the austere Gothic **Claustro de Dom Afonso V** you have to walk outside the abbey to reach the octagonal **Capelas Imperfeitas** (Unfinished Chapels) on the east end. These were commissioned in 1437 by Dom Duarte (eldest son of João and Philippa) as a mausoleum but were completely transformed by Dom Manuel's master of works, Mateus Fernandes, into an extraordinary piece of Manueline creativity. Fernandes intended to build an upper octagon but work was abandoned when Dom Manuel turned his attention to his own mausoleum at Belém. The result is a strangely moving arena, open to the skies, with Fernandes' masterpiece, the huge western portal, dominating all with its carvings of thistles, ivy, flowers, interwoven patterns and, in the words of Beckford, all kinds of 'scollops and twistifications'. Even if you see nothing else in Batalha, you should not miss this.

Leiria, 11 kilometres (seven miles) north of Batalha, makes a convenient base for excursions to all the major monuments in the region. It is a pleasant, lively place on the River Lis, with a core of old streets below an eye-catching castle (open 9 am–7 pm), originally built in 1135 and partly restored.

Stay away from **Fátima**, 22 kilometres (14 miles) southeast of Leiria, on the 12th of May and October. This is when over 100,000 pilgrims head for the famous sanctuary, one of the most important in the Catholic world since an apparition of the Virgin appeared here to three young shepherd girls on 13 May 1917 and on the 13th of the following five months. It is not a tourist site—'leave outside the curiosity and the manner of dress proper to a tourist', says a sign at the entrance—but rather a 'time and place of prayer'.

Throughout the year, thousands of supplicants daily cross a huge esplanade on their knees (some even supporting a child in one arm) to reach the **Chapel of the Apparitions** and a vast white **Basilica** housing the tombs of two of the girls. (The third, the only one who was able to converse with the Virgin, is a nun in Coimbra.) Despite the crowds, you never hear a voice raised; only a low murmur of prayer ripples from the Chapel as smoke rises from the constant burning of wax offerings.

Tomar and Around

If Fátima is today's religious stronghold, **Tomar**, 34 kilometres (21 miles) east, was yesterday's. It was here that the Order of the Knights Templar—crusaders, and conquerors of the Moors—first established their headquarters in 1160. Disbanded in 1314, they reasserted their power under the Order of Christ, and their **Convento de Cristo** at Tomar (open 9.30 am–12.30 pm, 2–6 pm, closed Monday) became an artistic symbol of their influence and status.

The twelfth-century, 16-sided **Charola**, based on the Holy Sepulchre in Jerusalem, makes a fascinating entrance to the complex. But it is the Manueline **window of the Chapter House** that takes the cake at Tomar. Best seen from the terraces of the Santa Barbara cloister, adjacent to the Main Cloisters, this is the purest example of the influence of the Age of Discoveries on Manueline art: the window is a mass of marine motifs, including intricately carved seaweed, coral, coils and cables, topped by the Order's Cross of Christ (which was emblazoned on all the discoverers' ships). The **Main Cloisters** carry the hallmarks of the next artistic era—the Renaissance—with Tuscan columns, Ionic pillars and sinuous stone stairways.

On the Grand Tour

*T*hus far have we pursued our route, and seen all sorts of marvellous sights, palaces, convents, &c.—which, being to be heard in my friend Hobhouse's forthcoming Book of Travels, I shall not anticipate by smuggling any account whatsoever to you in a private and clandestine manner. I must just observe that the village of Cintra in Estramadura is the most beautiful, perhaps in the world. . .

I am very happy here, because I loves oranges, and talk bad Latin to the monks, who understand it, as it is like their own,— and I goes into society (with my pocket-pistols), and swims in the Tagus all across at once, and I rides on an ass or a mule, and swears Portuguese, and have got a diarrhoea and bites from the mosquitoes. But what of that? Comfort must not be expected by folks that go a pleasuring.

When the Portuguese are pertinacious, I say, "Carracho!"— the great oath of the grandees, that very well supplies the place of "Damme,"—and, when dissatisfied with my neighbor, I pronounce him "Ambra di merdo." With these two phrases, and a third, "Avra Bouro," which signifieth "Get an ass," I am universally understood

A view of Sintra (below) and its famous Pena Palace (left)

to be a person of degree and a master of languages. How merrily we lives that travellers be!—if we had food and raiment. But, in sober sadness, anything is better than England, and I am infinitely amused with my pilgrimage as far as it has gone.

Lord Byron in a letter to Francis Hodgson, 1809

The town of Tomar makes an enjoyable stopover with its rambling parks and rose-clad back-streets. In one of these, at 73 Rua Joaquim Jacinto, you will come across an intriguing bit of history—a fifteenth-century **synagogue**. This is one of only two monuments of medieval Jewry in Portugal that have survived (the other is at Castelo de Vide), although it was subsequently used as a prison, chapel, hay-loft and warehouse until classified as a National Monument in 1921. Now run as a Luso-Hebraic Museum by Luís Vasco (he lives at no. 104 and has the key if it is closed), it houses some historical remains as well as the corner-stone of Belmonte's former synagogue. Vasco plans to install a glass floor over the women's ritual baths discovered next door.

A delightful afternoon's excursion from Tomar is the twelfth-century **Almourol Castle**, 22 kilometres (14 miles) south. Billed as Portugal's most romantic castle, it stands alone on a rocky island in the Tagus River. An old man ferries you across in a blue and white boat (Es.100 or so round trip), patiently waiting under the willows while you climb the castle walls.

Santarém, 65 kilometres (40 miles) south of Tomar, offers a more macho image as a centre for bullfighting. But once you have mastered its dastardly one-way streets, you will actually find the town quite charming, thanks to the sixteenth-century **Marvila Church** with its pretty azulejos, and the **Archaeo-logical Museum**, a one-nave jumble of assorted relics housed in a former church. Among the cooing pigeons, bits of carved stone, and headless painted wooden saints, look out for a glass case containing a decayed tooth—the only bit left of Duarte de Menses after an obviously ferocious fight against the Moors in 1464.

Caldas da Rainha and Around

The fame of **Caldas da Rainha**, 51 kilometres (32 miles) west of Santarém, was established by Queen Leonor, wife of Dom João II. She was so impressed by a chance encounter with the sulphuric waters here that she sold her jewels and lace to found a hospital and baths on the site in 1485. The spa hospital has been popular ever since (step inside its entrance in Largo Rainha Dona Leonor for a potent sulphuric sniff), though the town's tourist interest now centres more on its **Saturday market**, full of quivering rabbits, disgruntled hens, swathes of flowers, and the local cabbage-leaf pottery.

Óbidos, five kilometres south of Caldas da Rainha, rivals Marvão as the prettiest walled village in Portugal. Óbidos has the edge, though this also means more tourists. Stay the night to see the village at its quietest and best. Once commanding the seashore, Óbidos was won from the Moors in 1148 and refortified so attractively that Dom Dinis gave it to his wife as a bridal gift—a royal tradition that lasted until 1833. It still has a romantic touch, the terracotta-roofed houses wrapped by wisteria, honeysuckle and bougainvillea. In the

museum (open 9 am–1 pm, 2–6 pm, closed Monday) there is a portrait by Josefa de Óbidos, a famous seventeenth-century artist who spent most of her life here.

The Coast

Nazaré, 34 kilometres (21 miles) southwest of Leiria, is the most famous resort in Estremadura, though not the best. In fact, this formerly traditional fishing village has burst the bubble of its success: off-season, visitors are hassled to take rooms by the tough local women, and in-season they are hard pushed to find any rooms at all, harrassed instead to buy pistachios and fish-net trinkets for their cars. Tourists and seagulls strut along the still-perfect beach and screaming kids take the **funicular** to the older district of **Sítio** where buses disgorge more tourists for the panoramic views, more pistachios and pottery.

In total contrast, **Praia da Foz do Arelho**, some 26 kilometres (16 miles) south, where the Obidos lagoon meets the sea, has few tourists, few hotels and a great expanse of sand, with the bonus of calmer swimming in the lagoon. The only drawback is lack of shade. A spectacular high coastal road leads 14 kilometres (nine miles) north to **São Martinho do Porto**, with its horsehoe bay of brilliant blue. But its calm, warm waters are now well known; go off-season to enjoy its charms.

North of Nazaré stretches a vast pine forest initiated by Dom Dinis in the thirteenth century as a bulwark against the encroaching sand. The **Pinhal Real** now covers almost 10,000 hectares (39 square miles) and is one of the most beautiful stretches of the Estremaduran coastline, giving shade to the low-key, purpose-built resort of **São Pedro de Muel** with its streets of villas and excellent campsite. Further north, beware of water pollution from paper factories.

Off the Track

For an alternative to the thundering traffic of the N109 between Leiria and Figueria da Foz, take the coastal route through **Pinhal do Urso**. The way is rough, but worth every pothole for the scent of pines and the quiet company of ponies and carts, laden with logs from the forest.

Just eight kilometres (five miles) south of Batalha, the pretty little town of **Porto de Mós** is surrounded by the smooth hills of the Serra d'Aire that hide a handful of **caves**. **Mira d'Aire** (open 9 am–6 pm, until 9 pm in July and August) is the most popular, using dramatic lighting and fountain effects to enhance huge caverns. Speleologists may also enjoy the nearby Grutas (caves) de Alvados and de Santo António.

Dom Dinis: King of the Castle

Castles crop up everywhere in Portugal. And linked to most of them is the name of Dom Dinis. The son of Dom Afonso III, Dinis ruled from 1279 to 1325 and made defences his speciality, building or rebuilding over 50 castles, particularly along the strategic eastern frontier with Spain. The fortresses of Elvas, Marvão, Pinhel and Almeida are some of the more formidable examples which helped secure Portuguese independence even centuries after Dinis' death.

Many of the castles are on the site of earlier Moorish, Roman or even Visigothic fortifications and tend to share similarities in design, with double perimeter walls encircling a square keep *(Torre de Menagem)*, elaborate balconies and detailed machicolations. Holes for pouring down boiling oil (as clearly seen in the keep at Estremoz) were another feature of the time. Sometimes, however, Dom Dinis went for something quite unique, like the heptagonal *Torre de Galo* (Cockerel's Tower) at Freixo de Espada-à-Cinta.

But Dinis was more than a castle-maker. He was also a talented poet, an excellent administrator and far-sighted ruler: he brought the judicial systems under royal control, reformed the dangerously powerful Knights Templars into the Order of Christ, boosted agriculture and trade by establishing 40 'free fairs' and founded the first university in Lisbon in 1290.

So as well as enjoying the Castle King's beautiful fortresses at Óbidos, Monsaraz and Almourol (the most romantic castle of all, set on its own island in the River Tagus), you can also thank Dom Dinis for the splendid pine forest *(Pinhal Real)* north of Nazaré which he planted as a bulwark against encroaching sand and to provide wood for shipbuilding. It covers some 10,000 hectares (39 square miles) and is one of the most serene stretches of the Portuguese coastline.

The Beiras

Covering nearly all the land between the Douro and Tagus rivers, the Beiras are divided into Coastal, Lower and Upper provinces. They hold an incredible diversity of landscape, from pine-backed dunes, lagoons and sandy beaches to the country's highest mountain range, the Serra da Estrêla. Here is the cradle of Portugal's independent spirit, where the tough Lusitani fought it out against the Romans, while nearer the coast is the country's former capital—Coimbra—with its oldest university.

The more mountainous areas are sparsely populated, with remote villages depending on sheep and goats, and their crops of wheat, rye, vines and maize. Off-the-track discoveries here are among the most dramatic in the country.

Beira Litoral (Coastal)

Coimbra, the most distinguished city in the Beiras, was the country's capital from 1143 to 1255, and home of its first and most prestigious university, founded in 1290. Clambering around a high hill above the River Mondego, the old town suffers these days from busy traffic and unsightly modern developments but once you have managed to find a parking space (a challenge for the best brains), you will find the lively university atmosphere, ancient alleys and monuments an intoxicating mix. You can add a sentimental strain, too: Coimbra is famous for its own intellectual brand of *fado*, the uniquely Portuguese laments sung to 12-string guitars.

The old **university** at the top of the hill is centred around a courtyard with one side open to fine views over the River Mondego. Up the grand stairway to the right, a door marked 'reitoria' leads to the **Sala dos Capelos** (open 9.30 am–12.30 pm, 2–6 pm), the ceremonial hall where degrees are conferred. Its seventeenth-century painted ceiling and sober portraits of kings are less memorable than the view from the catwalk at the side.

Loitering tour groups outside doorways (you have to ring and wait to be let in) indicate the university's other attractions: the Manueline **chapel** with its flamboyant baroque organ, and the 1724 **library**, a gilded hall with imitation marble walls, Chinoiserie paintwork, and tables inlaid with ebony and jacaranda. The guide repeats a standard patter and expects a tip.

Downhill a little from the university, in the former episcopal palace, is the **Machado de Castro Museum** (open 10 am–12.30 pm, 2–5 pm, closed Monday), one of the best in the country, especially for its sculpture. Coimbra initiated a renowned school of sculpture in the sixteenth century, using local Ança stone and influenced by resident French and Italian artists. The Frenchman, Nicholas Chanterène, was one—his *A Virgem Anunciada* here is an inspired work. Among the paintings, look for the fifteenth-century *Ecco Homo* by Quentin Matsys with its faces of extraordinary cruelty, and the *Ascension* by the Master of Celas. The museum's basement is popular with children: a vast

98

Coimbra University's sumptuous Baroque Library and chapel organ (below);
The university city of Coimbra overlooking the River Mondego (right)

network of Roman vaulted galleries, great for playing hide-and-seek.

Heading down into the tangled lanes, you cannot miss the **Cathedral**, or Sé. Students of architecture get hands-on lectures in this stout twelfth-century fortress-church, a fine example of the Romanesque whose sole concessions to flamboyance are huge shells for holy water and a gilded Gothic altarpiece.

More elaborate goodies are inside the sixteenth-century **Church of Santa Cruz** at the bottom of the hill on Coimbra's busiest shopping street, Rua Visconde de Luz. The Coimbra school produced some of its best works here, notably a beautiful pulpit (probably by Chanterène), tombs for the first two Portuguese kings and, through the sacristy with its great canvas by André Goncalves, a Cloister of Silence with carved reliefs.

While you are here, visit the **Café Santa Cruz** next door for an atmospheric cup of coffee: art nouveau touches (winged beasts holding lamps, mirrored walls and wood panelling) have been added to a vaulted monastic hall. At night, when the Praça do Comércio below has turned to shadows, the café's stained-glass windows glow like a beacon for Bohemian students.

Across the Santa Clara bridge lies Coimbra's weirdest sight: the drowned ruins of the fourteenth-century **Convent Church of Santa Clara-à-Velha**. Abandoned to the river's flooding for the past 300 years, the church is now surrounded by murky algae pools, its rose window at eye level, its nave echoing

with the croaking of frogs. Just beyond it is livelier entertainment: **Portugal dos Pequeninos** (open 9 am–7 pm) is a park of famous Portuguese monuments in miniature plus displays on the overseas colonies. The energetic can try a kayak down the river: available every day from 1 May to 15 October.

Just 15 kilometres (nine miles) southwest of Coimbra are the Roman ruins of **Conimbriga** (open 9 am–1 pm, 2–6 pm and until 8 pm in summer; museum open from 10 am; get there early to avoid the school tours). The most impressive Roman site in the country, its mosaics and baths date from the third century when Conimbriga was an important destination on the Lisbon to Braga road.

The massive wall that dominates the ruins was a hurried defence against invading barbarians, and cut the city in two. But after a Swabian attack in 465, Conimbriga was finally abandoned for safer Aeminius (Coimbra), and thereby preserved for our enjoyment. Buy a plan at the museum to appreciate the size of the place (much lies beyond the wall, still unexcavated) and spot the best mosaics, including a nautical centaur amidst dolphins and wading birds, to the right of the entrance.

Another popular excursion from Coimbra is to the **Forest of Buçaco**, 27 kilometres (17 miles) northeast. Not just any old wood, Buçaco is imbued with centuries of religious feeling. Benedictine monks first built a hermitage here 1,500 years ago and in 1628 the Barefoot Carmelites established a monastery in

the heart of the forest, introduced a variety of new trees ranging from Mexican cedars to Himalayan spruce, and enclosed it all within walls. Monks as well as trees were protected—women were forbidden to enter and anyone damaging the forest was threatened with excommunication.

Now everyone is welcome, even the French (Wellington defeated them here in 1910 in a major reverse for Napoleon). Maps are available at the delightful neo-Manueline **Palace Hotel**, built for the royal family in 1907 on the site of the monastery (only a chapel and cork-lined cloister remain next door). Strange to say, even on the noisiest holidays the forest seems unperturbed: with its little chapels and overgrown paths it has a deeply reflective air that seems to well from the very roots of its huge, exotic trees.

On the seaside, there is everything except introspection, although the major resort of **Figueira da Foz**, 40 kilometres (25 miles) west of Coimbra, comes as a very pleasant surprise—probably because its endless beach and lively casino soak up all the tourists. There is even a quiet area for picnics in the nearby **Serra da Boa Viagem**, a hill of cedar, pine and eucalyptus above Buarcos.

Head north another 29 kilometres (18 miles) to **Praia de Mira**, famous for its traditional method of bringing in fish-nets by teams of oxen. In fact, tractors now do most of the work but it is still a wonderful scene: the fishermen playing pranks on each other as the nets are slowly drawn into land and the rush of activity as the oxen are led up and down the beach for the last haul. Seagulls and fisherwomen gather as the bulge of fish drops onto the sand; while each little pile of sardines is auctioned off, another boat is pushed out on logs into the sea.

The most relaxing resort on the Atlantic coast is **Aveiro**, 26 kilometres (16 miles) north of Mira, at the edge of a huge estuary (Ria). Historically, Aveiro has had its ups and downs: from a thriving medieval seaport it declined after 1575 when the lagoon and harbour closed up. Only in 1808 was a passage to the sea finally re-established and prosperity restored.

Surrounded by salt marshes, beaches, and canals (some even entering the heart of town), Aveiro's aquatic setting is complemented by picturesque canal-side merchant and fishermen's houses. Several *barcos moliçeiros* (the low, flat-bottomed seaweed-collecting boats with prows gaily painted like a pack of cards) are often tied up in the central canal, below the **Turismo** (Praça da República). Day-long **boat trips** on the Ria start from this canal daily from 15 June to 15 September.

Aveiro has only one major sight as such: the **Regional Museum** (Rua Santa Joana, open 10 am–12.30 pm, 2–5 pm, closed Monday). This was formerly the Convent of Jesus, founded in 1465, seven years before the saintly Princess Joana, daughter of Dom Afonso V, made it her puritan home, refusing marriage to Richard III of England. Her tomb of Florentine marble mosaics is the convent's pride, though the eighteenth-century church comes close in richness. An often-reproduced fifteenth-century portrait of Saint Joana attributed to Nuno Gonçalves, and a striking sixteenth-century *Senhora da Madressilva* (Virgin with Honeysuckle), are among the museum's items. The room where Saint Joana died is now a poignant little chapel, gilded, painted and guarded by kneeling angels.

Aveiro has a good choice of **beaches**, all a bus-or car-ride away (Turismo has bus timetables). **Costa Nova** is perhaps the prettiest, with its striped beach houses and its lagoon-side fish restaurants. **Barra** is more popular with the young (Visual Café is the trendiest hang-out); the long stretch of sand, backed by tufted dunes and one of the tallest lighthouses in Europe, looks appealing enough, but the surf is suspiciously frothy (something to do with the nearby paper factory, perhaps?).

Overall, **São Jacinto** is probably your best bet. Accessible by bus and ferry (fun, but just enough trouble to keep the hordes away), it has a sprinkling of restaurants along the quay and, 15 minutes' walk the other side of town, a vast expanse of sand. The **Reserva Natural das Dunas de São Jacinto** (one kilometre north on Torreira road, open 9 am–5 pm), is a 666-hectare (2.5-square mile) reserve of pine forest with a set trail to the beach and back, and two bird-watching hides overlooking ponds (there used to be egrets here but they perversely left the year the area was declared a nature reserve). This is one of the few protected sand-dune areas left in Portugal.

Beira Alta (Upper) and Baixa (Lower)

The **Serra da Estrêla** (now a National Park) is a great mountain barrier in the heart of Portugal, throwing up the country's highest peak, the Torre, to a height of 1,990 metres (6,530 feet). Valleys of maize and rye look up to pines and oaks and wild flowers. At the top are rough boulders and a flurry of snow in winter; there is even some skiing, though hiking is a more reliable and rewarding activity. Two of the best bases for this are **Penhas da Saúde** and **Covilhã** from where you can tackle the Torre, an easier climb than you might expect.

Viseu, the capital of the Beira Alta, lies northwest of the range, 85 kilometres (53 miles) inland from Aveiro. It is a gracious little place for a capital, still proud of its most famous resident—Vasco Fernandes (known as 'Grão Vasco', 'great Vasco'), the sixteenth-century painter who, together with Gaspar Vaz, fuelled a highly influential Viseu school of painting.

It is the works of this school that make the **Museu Grão Vasco** (Praça da Sé, open 9.30 am–12.30 pm, 2–5 pm, closed Monday) so outstanding, particularly because of Vasco's Renaissance-style *St Peter on His Throne* and the 14 panels (a joint work by Vasco and students) that once adorned the cathedral's altar. One of the panels, the *Adoration of the Magi,* has an international touch, with the African King transformed into an Indian from recently discovered Brazil.

Beside the museum (formerly the Bishop's Palace) is the originally Romanesque **cathedral**. The most eye-catching feature inside is the vaulting, carved together with huge knots which look as if they are just waiting to be untied. The *coro alto* has a chubby angel musician below a sixteenth-century Brazilian

Candy-striped seaside cottages at Costa Nova, just south of Aveiro

lectern, her rosy wooden cheeks probably pinched by centuries of unangelic choir boys. On the first floor of the Renaissance cloisters is the **Cathedral Museum**, its jumble of exhibits (everything from a twelfth-century gospel to a Saint Isabel statue with a chignon hairdo) put into jolly perspective by a custodian who likes to practise jokes and disappearing tricks. Watch your watch.

The streets below the cathedral are the ones to head for to delve into Viseu's character. Renaissance houses with coats of arms and occasional Manueline windows are found in narrow lanes busy with shops (cheese freaks should visit **Casa dos Queijos** in Travessa Escadinhas da Sé, off Rua Direita). The old Jewish quarter around Rua Nova and Rua Augusto Hilarico is the most fascinating, with cobblers, frame-makers and workers' wine bars. Good restaurants are here, too—try the local red Dão wines, among the best in the country.

The capital of Beira Baixa, **Castelo Branco**, could not be more different. The wide streets and lack of ancient monuments are evidence of successive attacks from the nearby frontier, just 18 kilometres (11 miles) away. Even the ruined hilltop castle has been eclipsed by a surrounding garden viewpoint, the **Miradouro de São Gens**.

If you like gardens, head for the eighteenth-century garden of the former **Bishop's Palace**, a jovial little place of well-trimmed box hedges, spouting fountains and assorted statues, including a famous stairway of kings and apostles. The palace itself now houses the **Regional Museum** (open 9.30 am–12.30 pm, 2.30–5 pm, closed Monday) with superb eighteenth-century *colchas* (locally-made silk-embroidered bedspreads) among its collection of Roman remains, Flemish tapestries, old looms and sixteenth-century paintings.

The highlight in the dreamy flat lands of lower Baixa is, perhaps inevitably, a remote hilltop village; in fact, **Monsanto** would be a highlight anywhere. It is an extraordinary place, approached from Castelo Branco, some 50 kilometres (31 miles) to the southwest, through villages whose streets are green with grass, and where hoopoes often fly. Monsanto appears high above the plain, its granite houses camouflaged against the grey grain of the hill, huddled under the ruins of a massive castle.

Tour buses do reach here, but with only a couple of cafés and a small inn still under construction it remains cut off from the world, both practically and spiritually. Most of the centuries-old cottages remain incredibly primitive, hewn out of rock and housing as many hens, pigs and donkeys as humans. The younger people have long since left, and many cottages, as well as the *gruta* cavern where the men used to drink, have been abandoned.

But some old men still ride out on their mules to tend a few fields, while the old women apologise (in Monsanto dialect) for not accompanying you on the steep walk to the castle (last rebuilt by Dom Dinis 700 years ago) where there are stone tombs carved into the living rock, and a view to equal any in the land.

Instead, your guide may be a young Lisboan, José Reinaldo, one of several 'outsiders' to have fallen under the Monsanto spell, buying cottages (some no more than one-room huts) and delving into Monsanto history. A route through the village is impossible to describe—in the twisting alleys, instinct leads. If you are lucky, you will stumble on a Roman font inscribed 'this has slaked the thirst of many heroes', among circular pig-pens and rock-grey huts. Secrets abound in this hilltop fortress; to leave most undiscovered is part of the magic.

Nothing comes close afterwards. But full marks for trying go to the high walled village of **Castelo Rodrigo**, 72 kilometres (45 miles) northeast of Guarda, which has some of the same mystery and drama. Its hilltop manor house was burned down in the sixteenth century by villagers appalled that their marquis had helped Philip II of Spain seize the throne of Portugal. Now its ruins overlook sleepy lanes of rose-clad cottages, with teasing hints at history: there is a Rua Sinagoga (now housing hen-huts) and, in Rua da Cadeia (Prison Street), a pretty cottage sports a curious lintel of Arabic writing.

Off the Track

Alpedrinha, 12 kilometres (eight miles) southeast of Fundão, is in this section not because it is off the main road—it could not be more on it—but because few people think of stopping here. It certainly does not look very fascinating at first, but climb up above the road (follow Rua Antonio José Salvado Motta) and you will find an elaborate font, the **Chafariz de Dom João V,** dated 1714: the king commissioned it when he happened to pass by and tasted the town's excellent waters. The ruined Palácio de Picadeiro above, with turrets still standing was one of the grand houses that followed this sign of royal esteem.

Fonts and water give **Castelo Novo**, a few kilometres south, its appeal. The village, backed by hills, gushes water at every corner (bottled as *Alardo*, it is known for its curative powers). The pillory square is a lovely place, with cobbled streets leading to a ruined tower and water running from every pore.

Idanha-à-Velha, 12 kilometres (eight miles) southwest of Monsanto, is a forgotten village which was once a major Roman and Visigothic city. The reason for its downfall is odd: apparently a plague of tenacious rats forced the residents to flee. Or was it ants? At any rate, only a tumble of ruins and an ancient basilica remain, and Roman walls rising up above a huddle of houses.

Piódão is not a total secret (the village is on tourist posters and has attracted architectural heritage societies) but the journey alone will separate real discoverers from beach bums. This tiny mountain village, high in the Serra de Açor (on the fringe of the Serra da Estrêla), is distinguished by its almost untouched traditional appearance: a cluster of grey shale houses above a valley of terraced fields. It is a good two-hour drive from Coimbra on high and winding roads, but as soon as Piódão shimmers into view, hazy in the green valley below, you know you have found something special.

Gothic, Baroque and Twistifications

Sometimes you can have too much of a good thing: see one too many of Portugal's baroque church interiors with their ornate gilded woodwork, brimming with cherubs and grapes, and you will feel sated. Fortunately, there is plenty of variety to balance your intake: the earlier Gothic style (dominant from the twelfth to the sixteenth centuries) provides the perfect alternative to the baroque. The dramatically austere Gothic interior of the Abbey of Alcobaça, for instance, could not be a greater contrast to such baroque gilded 'greats' as Santo Antonio at Lagos or the Convent of Jesus at Aveiro.

The Abbey of Alcobaça is one of the finest examples of Cistercian architecture in Europe. Begun in 1178, it reveals strong French influences in its soaring simplicity and lightness. Its plan, in fact, is very similar to the Cistercian abbey of Clairvaux in Burgundy. But by the time work started on the Batalha Abbey over a century later, Portuguese Gothic had taken on a medley of European styles.

Portuguese, Irish and French architects all worked on Batalha; the combination of their imaginations and the changing architectural fashions of their times makes the Abbey the most stimulating Gothic building in Portugal. The fourteenth-century tombs of Dom Pedro and his lover Inês de Castro (both in Alcobaça Abbey) are the sculptural equivalents of Batalha's mature Gothic masterpiece.

Other Gothic creations in Portugal are the lovely cloisters attached to some

An elaborate arch in the cloisters of Batalha Abbey (above);
the fantastic Triton-supported window of Sintra's Pena Palace (below)

107

monasteries and churches, dozens of
impressive castles (those of Almourol,
Monsaraz, Óbidos and Bragança are the
most picturesque) and simple stone
doorways in many old towns. On the
painting scene, the most brilliant contribu-
tion was from Nuno Gonçalves, whose
Panels of St Vincent (now in the Museu
de Arte Antiga, Lisbon) provide a remarkably realistic portrait of leading figures of
the time.

But the most memorable style of art and
architecture in Portugal is its very own
creation—the Manueline. Marking the
transition from Gothic to Renaissance, the
Manueline refers to the style that flourished
during the reign of Dom Manuel I (1495–
1521). This was the time of the Great
Discoveries—Vasco da Gama landed on the
coast of India in 1498, Pedro Alvares
Cabral discovered Brazil in 1500, and by
1513 the Portuguese had reached Timor
and China.

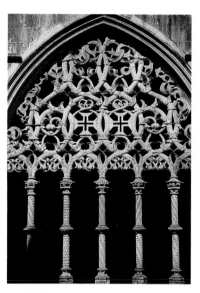

The confidence in the sea and the
exuberance of the age is displayed in stone
decoration of extraordinary inventiveness,
drawing heavily on nautical themes: coral,
ropes, seaweed, anchors and cables in
twisted stone accompany the ubiquitous
armillary spheres (Dom Manuel's emblem)
and the Cross of the Order of Christ (the
logo for the discoverers' ships). Architectural styles soar up like ocean waves, with
high network vaulting, aisles reaching to the
sky amidst a plethora of spiral decoration,
'scollops and twistifications', in the words
of the eighteenth-century English novelist,
William Beckford.

The masterpieces of this Manueline
style are the Jerónimos Monastery at Belém
and the window at the Convent of Christ in

Tomar. But even civic houses joined in the craze for Manueline motifs around doors and windows; you will catch sight of these as far afield as Viana do Castelo, Viseu and Évora.

Look out, too, for another important influence on Manueline art and architecture: Moorish *(mudéjar)* crafts, especially in carved wood ceilings and *azulejos* imported from Seville (Dom Manuel's extensions to the Royal Palace at Sintra are among the finest examples). Sintra is something of an exception, for most *mudejar* creations from this time are found in the Alentejo province, which attracted many Moorish artists from neighbouring Andalucia. In painting, the major Manueline artists were centred in Viseu under the leadership of Vasco Fernandes (known as Grão Vasco) and Gaspar Vaz. Their best works, characterized by brilliant colours and portraiture, can be seen in the Viseu Museum.

From the Manueline, Portugal rather reluctantly steered towards the Renaissance, guided by French sculptors such as Nicholas Chanterène and Jean de Rouen who settled in Coimbra (their pulpit at Coimbra's Church of the Holy Cross is a gem), and Spanish and Italian architects such as Diogo de Torralva and Filipo Terzi. Another major foreign influence continued to come from Flemish artists (Frei Carlos was one of the earliest and most important) as a result of close commercial ties between Lisbon and the Low Countries.

But when Portugal had regained its independence in 1640 after Spanish domination, and enthusiastically embraced the baroque style with all its unrestrained abundance, something really impressive reappeared on the artistic scene. The fact that the country was incredibly rich at this time (gold and diamonds had been discovered in Brazil), and Dom João V, an extravagant and liberal monarch, helped to create masterpieces of mind-boggling opulence such as the Chapel of St John the Baptist in Lisbon's Church of São Roque.

In the north, an inventive Italian influence predominated (particularly with Nicolau Nasoni's *Solar de Mateus* in Vila Real and Church of Clérigos in Oporto) as well as a fondness for ornamental rococo fantasies (best demonstrated by the monumental staircase of Bom Jesus).

But it was the uniquely Portuguese fad for *talha dourada*, gilded woodwork, that is the most obvious facet of this lavish baroque era. Thousands of pounds of gold leaf from Brazil were used to adorn carved altarpieces, pulpits, choir stalls and organ-cases in churches throughout the land; Oporto's Church of São Francisco (so distracting in its richness it is no longer used as a church) is one of the most awesome, with different styles of *talha dourada* ranging from high baroque to rococo. This indulgence in gilt, and the craze for *azulejos* which reached its peak at the same time, are aspects of Portuguese art and architecture which you are unlikely ever to forget.

The North

The Douro

A beautiful Scene it was!—& is!—The High land of Portugal, & the Mountain land behind it, & behind that fair Mountains with blue Pyramids & Cones. By the Glass I could distinguish the larger Buildings in Oporto, a scrambling City, part of it seemingly walls washed by the Sea, part of it upon Hills at first view, it looked much like a vast Brick kilnery in a sandy clayey Country, on a hot summer afternoon. . .

S T Coleridge, in a letter to Robert Southey, *16 April 1804.*

Even southerners admit that the north of Portugal—the Minho and Douro provinces—is the most beautiful part of the country, with its wooded hills and terraced vineyards, moist green valleys and rugged mountains. Named after their two major rivers, these are densely populated provinces, particularly the Douro Litoral around Oporto, the country's second largest city (and seen with Oporto eyes, its most important). The Alto (Upper) Douro is where the famous port wine grapes are grown—in terraced hills of schist and granite where the extreme temperatures produce what the locals call 'nine months of winter and three months of hell'. The extensive vineyards rising steeply up from the broad river make the Douro valley one of the most dramatically picturesque in Portugal.

Oporto

Like Lisbon, Oporto is built on steep hills above a river—the Douro—but it does not take long to notice that Oporto buzzes in a way that Lisbon never does. This is the heart of the country's most important economic area where 80 percent of the manufacturing industry is based, and most of the largest private enterprises. Oporto folk are proud of their work ethic, quoting the famous saying: 'Coimbra sings, Braga prays, Lisbon shows off, and Oporto works.'

They do enjoy themselves as well, especially when it comes to eating and drinking. An Oporto businesswoman took great pleasure in telling me the local recipe for octopus ('boil first, then skin, and fry in olive oil. . .'), and the best ways to appreciate ports ('ruby with sardines, vintage with candlelight'). They may be mocked by Lisboans for favouring tripe, but the *tripeiros* have the last laugh, calling Lisboans *alfacinhas*—lettuce-eaters. There is little love lost between them.

Today's Oporto (the name means 'the port', though Portuguese usually drop the definitive 'o') is shabbier than its zest deserves, though for tourists it is an atmospheric shabbiness: nineteenth-century granite buildings look down on a riverside area of tangled streets, flapping with laundry, smelling of fish. Even at

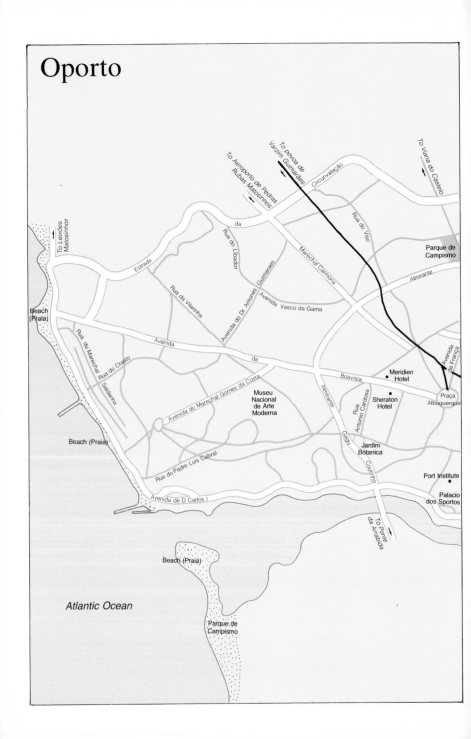

Oporto

To Leixões Matosinhos

To Aeroporto de Pedras Rubas Matosinhos

To povoa de Varzim Guimarães

Circunvalação

To Viana do Castelo

Rua do Viso

Parque de Campismo

da

Marechal Carmona

Almirante

Rua do Libador

Estrada

Rua da Vilarinha

Avenida do Dr Antones Guimarães

Avenida Vasco da Gama

Beach (Praia)

Rua du Marechal Saldanha

Rua do Crasto

Avenida

da

Boavista

Meridien Hotel

Avenida da França

Praça Albuquerque

Avenida do Marechal Gomes da Costa

Museu Nacional de Arte Moderna

Almirante

Rua Antonio Cardosa

Sheraton Hotel

Beach (Praia)

Rua do Padre Luis Cabral

Gago

Jardim Botanica

Coutinho

Port Institute

Avenida de D Carlos I

Palacio dos Sportos

To Ponte da Arrabida

Beach (Praia)

Atlantic Ocean

Parque de Campismo

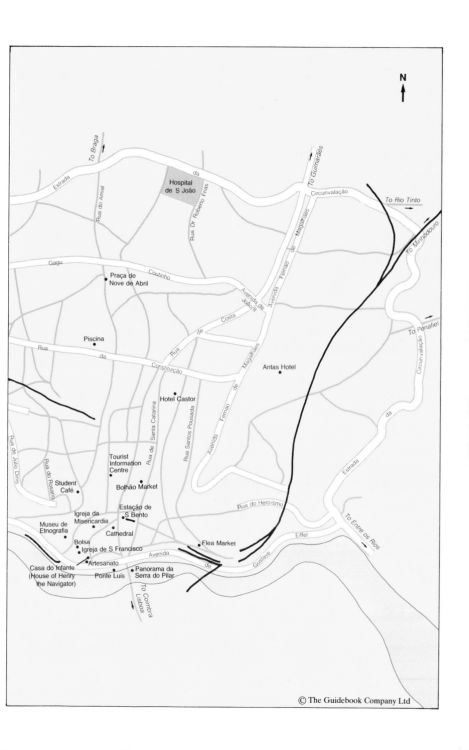

the heart of the smarter shopping and business district is the rambunctious
Bolhão Market, all cabbages and squawking hens, pigs and tripe and peaches.
Historic monuments are few; but Oporto is a great place just to wander, taking
in a visit to the famous port wine houses across the river.

Getting To and From

The best approach to Oporto is by **train**, crossing the Douro over the spectacular
Eiffel-designed Dona Maria Pia bridge. Most trains end up at **Estação de
Campanha** with regular connections to the central **Estação de São Bento**
(incidentally one of the most artistic in the country, with its hall of *azulejos*).
Some northern trains arrive at the nearby **Estação da Trindade**. You can reach
the **airport**, about 15 kilometres (nine miles) north, by bus 56 (at Jardim de
Cordoaria; allow 90 minutes) or taxi (approximately Es.1,500). The two main
bus companies are RN (Praça Filipa de Lencastre) for national routes, and
Cabanelas (Rua Ateneu Comercial do Porto) for northern services. Express
buses to Lisbon take about five hours; trains just over three.

Getting Around

Walking is your best bet—most of the major sights are centrally, if steeply,
located. **Buses** are fine, if you can work out their routes (the Turismo map is
little help); buying a block of tickets (*módulos*) or a Tourist Pass makes payment
easier—they are available at the *papelaría* on Avenida dos Aliados (near the
Café Imperial). There are fewer **trams** here than in Lisbon; the ones to the sea at
Foz and on to Matosinhos (no. 1 from Largo da Alfândega or no. 18 from Praça
Gomes Teixeira) offer the best rides.

A variety of **boat cruises** (from four hours to two days) up the Douro are run
by Endouro Turismo (49 Rua da Reboleira, tel. 02-324236) from March to
December. Their **'Three Bridges' cruise** is more expensive than the one run by
Ferreira port lodge. The latter costs Es.320 (tickets from the lodge in Vila Nova
de Gaia) but is unpredictable (supposedly every hour from 10 am to 6 pm except
Saturday and Sunday afternoon, but you may have to wait for a group tour). The
main **Turismo** office (across the Praça do General Humberto Delgado from the
post office) has good information, but the yellow dotted line on the pavement
leading to their sub-office in Praça Dom João I has long since faded. The sub-
office itself, however, is alive and occasionally kicking.

What to See

The best first stop in this naturally climbing and upwardly mobile city has to be
the top of the 75-metre (228 feet) **Torre dos Clérigos** (open 10.30 am to noon,
3–5 pm, closed Wednesday)—as fine a viewpoint as any city could wish for.
You can only really appreciate the Italian baroque style of the Church itself from
the bottom of Rua dos Clérigos. Another good city panorama is from the

cathedral, set above the cramped streets in real fortress style. Originally Romanesque, it was considerably remodelled in the eighteenth century but remains plain and rather claustrophobic. The seventeenth-century chased silver altarpiece in the chapel to the left of the altar is the only piece that sparkles.

From the cathedral square you can throw yourself down into the old town, following any twisting lane or stall-filled market street until you reach the river. Here are the grass roots of Oporto, houses so close and steps so steep you can peer into living rooms, budgies chirping in your ear, kids all out to play.

The **Cais da Ribeira** riverside has much the same intimacy though it is selling its charms to tourists now, too, with fancy riverside restaurants, and stalls of fruit and woollens. Henry the Navigator is said to have been born in a house in nearby Rua da Alfândega. (Oporto was more than a birthplace to the Prince— its shipyards also built many crusaders' fleets, in particular the one under his command which helped capture Ceuta from the Moors in 1415. It was the people's enthusiasm in supplying this fleet with all their beef and making do with the leftover tripe that explains their well-known affection for the stuff.)

Off the Rua da Alfândega is the **Centre of Traditional Arts** (37 Rua da Reboleira, open Tuesday to Friday 10 am–12.30 pm, 3–7 pm). Its renovated riverside house has a permanent exhibition and sales room—just the place to pick up a real genuine clay whistle, pigskin drum or pair of bellows.

A few minutes' walk uphill and you reach Oporto's most glittering work of art: the interior of the **Church of São Francisco** (open Tuesday to Saturday, 10 am–12.30 pm, 2.30–5 pm). It is no longer a functioning church, but its eighteenth-century extravaganza of gilt woodwork is over-the-top even as a museum. The rose window is the only simple feature left amongst cherubs, grapes, birds and laurels dripping with 90 kilos of Brazilian gold-leaf.

Next door is the rather more sober nineteenth-century **Bolsa** or Stock Exchange (open 9 am–noon, 2–5 pm, closed Saturday and Sunday afternoon) where prim guides whisk you through the Great Hall with its glass roof and coats of arms, up a carved granite staircase and through further lofty chambers, to the 'Arab Room', an imitation of the Alhambra which took 18 years and 18 kilos of gold to create. It looks like a jilted bride, all frills and no admirer.

Hidden in the Misericordia offices at 15 Rua das Flores is a **Fons Vitae painting**, one of the country's greatest Renaissance treasures, depicting in velvety colours Dom Manuel I, his wife Dona Leonor and their eight children around a fountain of blood from the crucified Christ. It is worth making a nuisance of yourself to get someone to show you this anonymous masterpiece.

Museums

The most important museum in town is the **Soares dos Reis Museum** (Rua de Dom Manuel II, open 10 am–noon, 2–5 pm, closed Monday), named after the famous nineteenth-century sculptor and featuring a number of his best works in

Portugal's Jewish Heritage

Portugal has been a home to Jews for over a thousand years. They first settled here in the time of the Moors and came to wield considerable power and influence as bankers, financiers, court doctors, astronomers and treasurers. The Afonsine Ordinance of 1446 ruled that they must live in segregated Jewish quarters (*Judiaria*), but compared to other European countries of the time, Portugal provided a relatively hospitable haven.

When Spain expelled its Jews in 1492, some 60,000 fled to Portugal, many settling in Guarda, Belmonte, Bragança, Tomar and Viana do Castelo. But only four years later, Portugal's Dom Manuel was forced to get tough as one of the conditions of his marriage to Princess Isabel of Castile. Reluctant to lose the Jews' financial expertise at a time of burgeoning wealth, Dom Manuel came up with a compromise: he demanded that the Jews be baptized as 'New Christians'. Not surprisingly, many refused, fled to Morocco or the Netherlands or continued to practise their faith in secret as *Marranos*, 'Hidden Jews'. Worse was to follow in the reign of João III who encouraged the Inquisition to persecute and burn to death thousands of 'New Christians' and *Marranos* during the sixteen6th and seventeenth centuries.

Today, although the remaining Jewish community is very small, traces of *Judiaria* can be found in many towns. The most famous is in Castelo de Vide where Portugal's oldest synagogue, founded in the thirteenth century, is tucked away in a narrow cobbled street.

Tomar, too, has a notable synagogue, dating back to the mid-fifteenth century. It served as a Jewish house of worship for only a few years before Dom Manuel ordered the Jews to convert. It was declared a National Monument in 1921 and is now a Luso-Hebraic Museum, containing evidence of Tomar's former Jewish community and the cornerstone of the famed thirteenth-century synagogue of Belmonte. The intimate, high-ceilinged hall is often used for concerts and cultural activities (jugs tucked into high niches in the walls improve the acoustics). Next door, where a library is planned, women's ritual baths have recently been discovered.

Many Portuguese probably have some Jewish blood following centuries of marriages between 'new' and 'old' Christians, but the largest community of Crypto-Jews numbers only about 450, and is found in Belmonte. Some are now going through a conversion process to return to Judaism.

More recent Jewish history is evident in Lisbon: a Jewish Community Centre, at 10 Rua Rosa Araújo, serves as a link between the original Sephardic Jews and Ashkenazi Jews who arrived as refugees in the mid-twentieth century. A Sephardic Synagogue, at 59 Rua Alexandre Herculano, houses historical documents and religious objects dating back to the fourteenth and fifteenth centuries.

bright and spacious galleries (*O Desterrado*, [The Exile], grabs your attention immediately). Among paintings from the same period, those by Silva Porto have a Corot-like dreaminess, while the young Henrique Pousão specialized in sentimental child portraits. There are some excellent early works—note, particularly, two women saints by Vasco Fernandes and a pensive sixteenth-century Trinity by Christovão de Fiqueiredo—as well as fine glassware and ceramics.

Much more absorbing, however, is the **Ethnography Museum** (Largo de São João Novo, open 10 am–noon, 2–5 pm, closed Sunday and Monday). Its curious odds and ends include a grape-press and old looms, nineteenth-century quills and inkpots, buttons and bows and cufflinks, and Oporto's first (turn-of-the-century) lift car.

Behind the Pálacio de Cristal gardens (now sporting a funfair), a cobbled street leads to the **Quinta da Macieirinha Romantic Museum** (open Tuesday to Thursday 10 am–12.30 pm, 2–5.30 pm, Friday and Saturday until 6 pm, closed Sunday morning and Monday), an odd little place dedicated to the exiled King Carlos Alberto of Sardinia who lived and died here in 1849. His moustachioed portraits dominate rooms of French Empire style furniture and a ballroom of jewellery, fans and dried flower displays.

A more lively part of the *quinta* can be found outside and down the steps to the **Solar do Vinho do Porto** (open 11 am–midnight, closed Sunday), an elegant airconditioned lounge for port-drinkers. The friendly waiters will help you choose from 152 varieties produced by 52 different firms, with prices ranging from a mere Es.80 for a glass of dry white to a respectable Es.17,000 for a carafe of vintage 1961.

Vila Nova de Gaia

When Oporto folk claim their region is the cradle of the country, they are not exaggerating. In Roman times, the important Lisbon to Braga route encouraged the development of settlements on both sides of the Douro River—Portus on the north, Cale on the south. It was this area of Portucale (which later came to include everything between the Minho and the Douro) that Henri of Burgundy gained as a dowry when he married Teresa, daughter of the King of Léon, in 1095. A focus of Christian revolt against the Moors, it gave its name to the new country that Teresa's son, Afonso Henriques, soon consolidated.

Today, the suburb across the river from Oporto is called **Vila Nova da Gaia** and is best known for the **port wine lodges** which stretch all along the river and up the hill above, dominating every view from Oporto with their giant white signs. Some of the traditional flat-bottomed *barcos rabelos* that used to carry the

port downstream from the Alto Douro vineyards add a more picturesque advertising touch along the quay, their sails billowing in the wind.

The easiest approach to Vila Nova is across the lower level of the nineteenth-century Dom Luís bridge from the Cais da Ribeira. But the upper level leads to the best viewpoint of Oporto: the **Monastery of Serra do Pilar** (used by Wellington to plan his crossing of the Douro in 1809 during the Peninsular War), from where you can glimpse vestiges of the old city wall.

Free tours and tastings at the lodge warehouses are a major tourist attraction these days, although you may find that some firms will only give group tours. Taylor's is one of the smallest and oldest companies (founded in 1692, in good time for the 1703 Methuen Treaty which opened up the English market to port wines) and gracious about taking even individuals around its lovely old premises, high above the river.

The quality of guides varies tremendously, but most will give you an idea of the process of port manufacture, and some—like the lady at Ferreira—may even be amusing ('I serve my port in a teapot, the old-fashioned way. You know why? Because it used to be considered unseemly for women to ask for port so they'd ask for "cold tea" instead, or "tea without steam". I'm like the English, I

Vinho Verdes, Ports and Wines

Portugal's most famous beverage—port—is a wine made only with grapes
grown in the Douro valley, fortified by the addition of grape brandy, and
matured in casks or large oak vats, traditionally at Vila Nova de Gaia.

The wine can be red or white (chilled white port with grilled sardines is
delicious) but it is the red, or ruby, port that most people know and love. This is
the commonest kind of port, sweet and full-bodied, made from a blend of lesser
wines, bottled early and drunk young. Tawny ports, from a selection of wines
which mature fairly early and consequently lose colour quickly, are kept in the
cask for at least seven years.

Most highly prized of all are the vintage ports, traditional after-dinner wines
(best drunk by candlelight, say the experts), made only in outstanding years,
and never mixed with other wines. After about two years in vats, vintage wine
is matured in black-coloured glass bottles in the cool, dark cellars of Vila
Nova's port lodges. It will take at least ten to 15 years to mature, and need
decanting, unlike the late bottled vintage port which is wine of a single year,
matured and bottled four to six years after it has been wood-aged in the vats
and immediately ready for drinking.

Although port is now enjoyed throughout Europe, it has traditionally found
its best market in England. 'The Portuguese and the English have always been
the best of friends,' quipped a Captain Frederick Marryat in 1834, 'because we
can't get no Port Wine anywhere else.' True enough, the exceptional conditions
under which port wine grapes are grown and ripened—an extreme
'microclimate' (described by locals as nine months of winter and three months
of hell), and a soil of schist which retains the heat of the day—are found
nowhere but along the Douro River, in the world's oldest demarcated wine-
growing area, established in 1756.

From as early as the thirteenth century British merchants who had settled in
Oporto to engage in the cloth and Newfoundland cod business had enjoyed and
promoted the wines of the Minho region (Viana do Castelo was the main export
base). But it was the tit-for-tat trade restrictions between France and England in
the late seventeenth century (no English cloth allowed into France and no
French wines into England) which spurred the British merchants of Viana and
Oporto into finding enough Portuguese wines to fill the gap.

A few adventurous souls like Peter Bearsley, son of the founder of Taylor
Fladgate & Yeatman, set off into the remote, inhospitable regions of the Upper
Douro. Here, in monasteries and humble farms (so the stories go), they found
some superb wines. Those of Lamego—'the most excellent and most lasting
ones to be found in the realm, as well as the most fragrant', according to a

sixteenth-century source—have a strong claim to being the original 'ambrosia of the north', but different merchants were soon exporting wines from all over the area.

In order to preserve the wines better on their journey to Oporto (originally in skins on mule-back) and to retain their sweetness, small doses of a fortifying brandy began to be added. With the 1703 Methuen Treaty favouring even further the market for Portuguese wines in England, business really took off; British shippers got greedy, all kinds of adulterants and colourants were added to the wine, quality suffered, and in 1756 the Marquis de Pombal stepped in. He demarcated the area for wine-growing and decreed that the Alto Douro Wine Company was to control the entire port-wine trade.

It upset the British no end, of course, but controversy was to flare even more bitterly in the 1840s when Joseph James Forrester arrived on the scene. An extremely talented young man, he produced the best maps of the Douro area ever to exist, wrote technical papers on grape diseases and then, to the horror of most merchants, criticized the practice of adulterating wines with too much brandy. He died in 1861 when his boat capsized on the Douro. The fortification of wines (essential in small quantities to produce port as we know it) continued unabated, although there are now strict controls and limits.

It was at this time that the British began buying *quintas*, or country estates among their vineyards in the Douro, to serve as seasonal offices and preliminary cellars—as they still do today. Originally, the wine was brought down the river to Oporto (in the March after the autumn harvest) in square-sailed *barcos rabelos*. Now transport is by more mundane road tankers and the only *barcos rabelos* to be seen serve as advertisements outside the port lodges in Vila Nova de Gaia.

Treading the grapes is a rare practice, too, these days (some firms retain it only for their very best grapes), although the harvesting work is still as hard as ever, with most terraced vineyards too steep and narrow for tractors. But that is slowly changing, thanks to European Community funding which is bringing more mechanization into the terraces.

It is probably only in Britain that more Portuguese port than wines are sold. But the regional wines are also excellent, whether it is a quality wine of limited quantity or a *vinho da casa*, an unbranded local wine always available in restaurants.

The best known are the *vinho verdes*, or 'green wines', so-called because they are drunk young (and because they come from the lush green Minho province). A light, slightly effervescent wine, *vinho verde* comes in both red and white, though the whites are generally preferable. For reds, try the full-bodied *Dão* from the Viseu region, tasting as velvety as a Burgundy, and similar to the *Pinhel* red further east.

The Lisbon area has long produced a famous red, too, the *Colares*, although urban development has encroached on the vineyards, a fate that has also affected the long-established nearby vineyards of Bucelas, Carcavelos and Sétubal. The latter produces a rich, sweet *moscatel*, a fortified wine from a blend of black and white grapes, perfect as a dessert wine. If you are passing through the heart of the port wine region, near Pinhão, stop at Favaíos for a bottle of the only other *moscatel* in Portugal, a delicious, little-known nectar.

One of the oldest quality wines of all, Madeira, is still a favourite. A unique wine because of the island's volcanic soil and the gradual heating method used (called *estufas*), Madeira is blended, matured, and fortified. It lives longer than any other wine in the world.

On a final note, you may like to try a wine that 'dies' longer than any other: a 'wine of the dead' *(vinho dos mortos)* produced only in Boticas, in the northern Trás-os-Montes province. The locals of this otherwise unremarkable village first buried their wine in 1809 to hide it from the invading French troops. Finding afterwards that it tasted rather better than before, they continued with the practice. This so-called 'wine of the dead' (now usually buried for just a year or two) is available at the village Café de Armindo.

can get through a pot of this tea a day, no problem!') There is no great pressure to buy, but all lodges have a sales counter in the hall where tastings are given (usually generous glasses of both red and dry white). Port is available every-where else in town as well.

The Douro Litoral

One of the busiest resorts on this Costa Verde—'green coast'—is **Póvoa do Varzim**, which is only worth visiting if you want to swim, gamble, or mix with other tourists. Quieter charms are available at nearby **Vila do Conde**, an easy 27-kilometre (17-mile), day trip north of Oporto (anything closer is polluted).

Still pursuing its traditional fishing and boat-building, Vila do Conde has a rural rather than resort atmosphere, with a huge open market opposite the **Turismo** office (Avenida 25 de Abril) offering mounds of flour-dusted loaves (bread is very popular in the north), socks and shoes and lace.

Nothing in Vila do Conde is bigger than lace (in line with the old Portuguese saying that 'where there's nets, there's lace'). You can find plenty of locally-made samples in the Turismo's **Handicraft Centre** (Rua 5 de Outubro, open 10 am–7 pm) but it is much more interesting to visit the **School of Lace-Making** in the former Convent of Carmo, near the attractive old boat-building area.

Some 50 four- to five-year-olds (including a couple of boys) are taught here by the town's best practitioners, such as Maria Beatrix Estrela Graça. 'You don't *have* to be so young to start learning,' says Maria, 'all you need are good eyes, patience and persistence.' The school was set up in 1918: 'there's no other school quite like this in Portugal,' she says, proudly, 'or, of course, lace quite as good.' Contact her on tel. 052-631255 if you want some private instruction.

Vila do Conde's other sights can be wrapped up in a half-hour break from the beach: the early sixteenth-century **Igreja Matriz** (parish church), with its elaborate Manueline portal; and, dominating the skyline with its personal aqueduct, the **Convent of Santa Clara** (now a liberal reformatory for a hundred teenage boys) whose fortress-style church contains beautifully-carved Renais-sance tombs of the founders.

Still within the Douro Litoral region, the enchanting town of **Amarante**, 56 kilometres (35 miles) east of Oporto, purrs beside the willowy Tâmega River. Visitors used to come here to ride the narrow-gauge Tâmega railway to Arco de Baúlhe. Now this sector has been axed (as well as services on the Vouga and Corgo Lines), in a short-sighted cost-cutting measure.

Amarante offers other pleasures, though, not least of which is sitting on the bougainvillea-clad balcony of the Hotel Silva and watching the river glide by. Down the street is the **Convento de São Gonçalo**, founded in 1540 and contain-ing the tomb of the saint in a tiny chapel on the left of the chancel. Thanks to his reputation as a marriage-maker, the saint's right toe has been rubbed away by those desperate for his magic touch in finding a partner, and his face worn and blackened by kisses. An air of hope still smothers the carnation-covered tomb, reinforced every first weekend in June when the **São Gonçalo fiesta** is celebrated with songs, dance and the traditional exchange of phallus-shaped cakes among Amarante's young men and women.

Behind the church, in the former cloisters, is the **Albano Sardoeira Museum** of modern art (open 10 am–12.30 pm, 2–5.30 pm, closed Monday), dominated by the works of Amadeo de Sousa Cardoso, Portugal's most famous modern painter, who was born locally.

An eighteenth-century bridge (with a plaque proudly commemorating a local stand against Napoleon's troops) leads to Rua 31 Janeiro where you will find several good restaurants and, at no. 102, a typical *tasca* (tavern) selling smoked hams, cheeses and red wines; sit and have a mugful, local-style, under hanging hams and laurel branches.

If Turismo had their way, Amarante would be recognized 'as one of the main poles of development, from the great road axis IP4 linking Oporto–Amarante–Vila Real–Bragança'. Luckily, there is still an alternative route to Vila Real: unless you are in a rush, avoid the IP4, whizzing along the mountain ridge, and dawdle instead on the wiggly, old N15. It winds through wooded hillsides, granite villages and farmsteads (where hay is hung from poles, and vines trained to grow as tall as trees), before climbing into the windswept heights of the Serra do Marão.

The Alto Douro and Douro Valley

The road to **Lamego** from Amarante crosses the Marão range, too, joining the Douro valley just before Peso da Régua, which is nine kilometres (five miles) north of Lamego and its nearest train station. Curiously underrated, Lamego and its environs contain some extraordinary treasures. You could happily potter around this quiet, hilly countryside for days. On the edge of the wilder Trás-os-Montes region, Lamego has some of that province's same sense of mystery.

It has always been something of a magnet, for centuries an important trading post and episcopal city where the first Portuguese parliament met in 1143. And it was here, so some say, that the original port wines—'the most excellent and most lasting ones to be found in the realm, as well as the most fragrant', according to a sixteenth-century source—were produced in monasteries, and discovered by visiting English merchants who snapped up this 'ambrosia of the north' during the early eighteenth century.

Pombal later built a road to Régua so that the Vinho de Lamego could more easily be shipped down the Douro to Oporto. Smoked ham and sparkling wines are now more famous local products (Lamego's Rua da Olaria has some of the best ham shops)—picnics here have real class.

The town itself is pretty classy, too, with streets of eighteenth-century bourgeois houses overlooked by twelfth-century castle ruins on one hill, and the

baroque **Church of N S dos Remédios** on another. Site of a major pilgrimage on 8 September, the church is approached by a zigzag stairway (like the one at Braga's Bom Jesus) leading up past *azulejo* panels from the town's central park. Marriage parties love the Square of Arabian Kings at the top, posing beside the fountain of bearded giants under the gaze of swashbuckling royal statues.

Down in the heart of things is the **cathedral**, once Romanesque and now mostly Renaissance. Its curious portal depicts drinking men and seahorses, and winged beasts devouring cherubs. To the left is an attractive Gothic cloister where schoolgirls like to play recorders. To the right, note the stonemasons' personal squiggles on the cathedral's bell-tower wall, which is best seen from the *pastelaria* in Travessa da Sé, stocked with sweet cakes originally created by the nuns of Chagas Convent.

Across the square, the former eighteenth-century episcopal palace now houses the **Municipal Museum** (open 10 am–12.30 pm, 2–5 pm, closed Monday), one of the best in the country. Particularly outstanding are several sixteenth-century Flemish tapestries and five paintings by Vasco Fernandes that were commissioned in 1506 as part of a polyptych of 20 for the cathedral. Other treasures are the fourteenth-century statues of a heavily-pregnant Virgin, and richly gilt baroque chapels transferred from the Chagas Convent. The *azulejo* panels from Lisbon's seventeenth-century Pálacio Valmor includes one that will appeal to hunters: it shows five-and-twenty magpies about to meet their end.

Lamego keeps its oldest sights up the hill around the **castle**; follow Rua da Olaria (beside the **Turismo**), past the **Church of Almacave** (so ancient it has sunk below street level) to a lane off Praça do Comércio that climbs into the citadel under the Porta dos Fogos. You may see boy scouts weeding the wall; they have been tidying up the place ever since the 1970s when they carted out 18 truckloads of rubbish from the keep. The keep is now a tidy armoury of boy scout paraphernalia, proudly displayed to you by a saluting boy scout guide.

But Lamego's most memorable places are on the fringes of town. One of these, the little **Chapel of the Exile** on the way to Balsemão, is easily overlooked. Few would guess that it is crammed with exquisite gilt woodwork, a coffered, painted ceiling and seventeenth-century *azulejos*. Through the old Bairro da Fonte neighbourhood below, follow the River Balsemão as it plunges down to the hamlet of **Balsemão** to find the **Chapel of São Pedro**, originally built by the Suevi in the seventh century. Various medieval additions were made by the Bishop of Oporto, Dom Afonso Pires. His carved sarcophagus, bright with sunshine falling on its angel wings, fills the curious little chapel.

The most relaxing way to enjoy the dramatic winding gorge of the **Douro valley** is by train from Oporto to Régua (or all the way to Tua—a journey of three-and-a-half hours—but check on services beyond Régua as they are slowly being cut back). The minor roads clinging to the riverside are a nightmare of traffic on holidays when all of Oporto seems to be out. Avoid exploring by car then, for this is one part of Portugal that deserves your undivided attention.

At the confluence of the Corgo and Douro rivers and their train lines, **Peso da Régua** marks the beginning of the world's oldest demarcated wine-growing region (established by Pombal in 1756). The hills are covered with terraced vineyards, providing spectacular views from **Miradouro de Boa Vista,** south of the river. Although **Pinhão**, 25 kilometres (16 miles) further east, is now recognized as the centre of quality port wine production, the industry's watch-dog body, the Casa do Douro, still has its headquarters in Régua.

Eastwards from Régua is the heart of port-land, where old company *quintas* (villas) are set amidst vineyards. Tractors are now being introduced to newly-widened terraces, but many areas remain inaccessible and can only be tended by han—a searing job in summer when temperatures often rise to 43°C (109°F).

A dramatic crossing of the Douro east of Pinhão is at **São João de Pesqueira**, where the steepest road you can imagine plunges to the Valeira reservoir and rises up again to Linhares, making your ears pop. The end of the valley, before the river curves north and becomes the border with Spain, is at **Barca d'Alva**, a remote, gentle spot nestling among hills of olives and almonds, a sheep's bleat away from Spain.

Off the Track

Close to Lamego are a trio of half-forgotten glories. The grandest is the **São João de Tarouca Monastery**, 12 kilometres (eight miles) south, tucked away in the Barossa valley. This was the first Cistercian monastery in Portugal, built in the early twelfth century and almost completely destroyed 700 years later when the religious orders were abolished. Only the church stands intact among the vast, eerie ruins of the monks' quarters; its Baroque interior harbours fine *azulejos*, gilt choir stalls and side chapels of notable early paintings. Two impressive fourteenth-century items lie in side aisles: the massive tomb of Dom Pedro, the bastard son of Dom Dinis; and a larger-than-lifesize granite statue of the Virgin and Child.

The nearby village of **Ucanha** seems unremarkable from the road, but follow the lane down to the river and you will find a huge, medieval fortified bridge. Stonemasons' initials are clearly visible on each block of stone. The old watermill by the reedy riverside is silent now and the stone laundry enclosures long since defunct, but washing still hangs under the arches, and folk still meet on the bridge above to watch the water chuckle by.

A few kilometres further is **Salzedas**, where a once-powerful, now-derelict Cistercian monastery looms over a nondescript village. Its church is green and black with mould, past hope of restoration. Services are still held here but the complex is rancid with decay. Sullen boys gather at the door, and slowly kick a football against the grey and lichenous wall.

Pillories, Pigs and Granaries

Nearly every town and village in Portugal has one: its *pelourinho* or stone pillory. Some are completely plain, others are ornately carved works of art. But for 500 years, from the thirteenth to eighteenth centuries, they served both as a form of punishment as well as a symbol of municipal power. Those who dispensed justice were allowed to erect a pillory for the purpose, which is why most pillories are found outside the town hall, cathedral or monastery, the most common seats of jurisdiction. The unfortunate criminals were chained from hooks at the top of the pillory (earlier versions had cages), or locked into attached hand-cuffs.

But craftsmen often thought more of art than punishment when building the pillories. Some of the most attractive Manueline examples have twisted columns topped by armillary spheres. The more unusual carry personal motifs, such as the pillory at Óbidos which bears a granite shrimping net, the symbol of Dona Leonor. The Gothic pillory at Barcelos has a hexagonal column with a graceful granite lantern, while the sixteenth-century marble pillory in Elvas is covered with strange stone dots. There are some curiously pagan-looking pillories in the northern mountain villages of Soajo and Lindoso which are carved with smiling faces, like a child's picture of the sun.

But these two villages are famous for something much more impressive: their collection of stone granaries, called *espigueiros*. A speciality of the Minho province, *espigueiros* are long granite coffers raised up on mushroom-shaped supports to keep vermin away from the maize and grain stored inside. With stone crosses on their roofs (symbolizing the sacredness of maize), they look disturbingly like coffins.

Individual *espigueiros* are dotted everywhere in the region, although not all of them stick to stone; some have corrugated iron covers, wood plank sides or brick supports. Some are as long as a house, others as small as a pig pen. And most of them, if the truth be known, are not all that effective against nibbling mice and rats. Peer inside those at Soajo to see for yourself.

So where do the pigs come into the picture? Once again, it is the north (especially the remote Trás-os-Montes region) that hosts these specialities in stone. The crudely carved granite boars or pigs known as *berrões* are prehistoric mysteries (some date back over 2,000 years). No-one really knows their original purpose, but they are believed to have either represented gods or served as offerings to the gods. The most famous one is at Murca, an otherwise unremarkable little town in Trás-os-Montes. Several others are in the museums of Chaves, Bragança and Miranda do Douro. But the most curious is inside Bragança castle: pierced through its middle is a plain *pelourinho*— perhaps representing the ultimate symbol of divine justice, or just a very odd pig indeed.

The Minho

Lying under the lid of Spanish Galicia, the northwestern province of the Minho is a moist, green land of densely-cultivated valleys, high granite ridges and sandy beaches, lashed by the cold Atlantic sea. This is no place for sunbathing; head inland, instead, to discover one of Europe's best kept secrets—a traditional world of lyre-horned oxen pulling creaking carts, yoked in pairs by ornamental wooden *cangas*; a world of country markets where villagers sell the fruits of their tiny plots of land; and a world of faith, with chapels and shrines at every turn and religious festivals every summer weekend.

The Minho is conservative, devout, and more obviously rural than anywhere else in Portugal, with smallholdings of maize and vegetables divided by low stone walls covered with trailing vines. The region's *vinho verde* is a sparkling young wine that contradicts the sense of age in this land of prehistoric hillforts and Romanesque churches.

The fancy new houses you see everywhere have been built by emigrant workers who flooded France and West Germany in the 1950s and 60s to relieve their poverty. Work opportunities have since shrunk, leaving many houses half-completed or turned into cowsheds, straw sticking out from their garish modern doors, pigs in the bedroom, donkeys in the yard.

But many villagers still live abroad, returning in August to flaunt their wealth. As a member of the European Community, Portugal must now tighten its belt and face increasing competition, and it is the *minhoto* peasants left behind who will suffer most. And the old, slow Minho province that will face the harshest changes.

Guimarães

The outskirts of the country's first capital are awful. Only when you reach the core of the old town do you begin to sense what once made it tick. Afonso Henriques, the first King of Portugal, was born here in 1110; 18 years later he fought his errant mother to protect Portuguese independence from Spain, and made Guimarães the power-base for his subsequent conquests of the Moors.

The pride of the place is centred in the **Largo da Oliveira**, a graceful medieval square bordered by the **pousada de N S da Oliveira** on one side, and the **Church of N S da Oliveira** with its Gothic canopy on another. An arcade leads through to the equally attractive **Largo de São Tiago**, bordered by houses dripping in colourful laundry and flowers. The **Rua de Santa Maria** runs under Moorish arches past both squares, with fifteenth-century mansions sporting elegant wrought-iron grilles.

You might expect the most memorable monument to be the hilltop **castle** (open 10 am–12.30 pm, 2–5 pm, closed Monday) where Afonso established his

Life and Death

With so much drinking, Manuel realized that he was getting tipsy. But his delight at finding himself back in his birthplace among his old companions made him forget himself and the world. He drank and drank, and after a little while he didn't know where he was. The ground danced under his feet. In drink, Louvadeus remained logical but tended to be melodramatic. And when he went in for high–flown thoughts it was impossible to sort out how much it all meant. Now his quarrel was with Justo.

'You don't know anything at all about life, friend!' he said. 'You're a fool! For you life is nothing but saving and hoarding! D'you want to know what life is? It's keeping afloat on the logs, over the river, and not getting your crupper wet or being carried off by the current. But if the current does take you, then keep your head high. What'd you do, Justo, if one moment you found yourself the owner of bags and bags of gold and the next stripped and penniless? Eh? What'd you do, Justo, if you found yourself with piles of money today, and you woke up tomorrow a pauper. Just tell me, what'd be the first thing you'd do, for I'd like to know what sort of man you are?'

'Well, that'd depend, Louvadeus. If I found myself poor today when I'd been rich yesterday, the first thing I'd do would be to scratch my head. I'd wonder: Well, how did it all come about?'

'And what then?'

'Then. . . I don't know. Then I'd try and mend matters. Let's imagine that my house was burned down. What could I do. . ?'

'And if you were robbed?'

'If I were robbed—if I were robbed, I'd shout for the police and chase after the thief.'

'You'd chase after the thief? And what if he had feet like a horse?'

'Ah, then I don't know what I'd do. . . If I could take a shot at him. . .'

'You'd take a shot at him. And what if you were to go after him unarmed?'

'Bah! All right, I don't know what I'd do! I don't know! He'd deserve a good fright!'

'You don't know? Oh, yes you do! Because you're tight-fisted and a miser. At bottom you're as bad as the man who robbed you. I know what you'd do, Justo my friend: if you got hold of him at the right moment you'd give him more than a good fright. . . you'd break his neck!'

The other started to laugh in order to take the sting out of these wild words, for Louvadeus was now quite drunk.

'Maybe. Anyway it'd be one rascal the less in the world.'

'But you'd have no right to kill him. A decent man doesn't kill his fellow, even if he's the worst kind of scoundrel. He doesn't kill, he doesn't.'

'Not if he's a peaceful soul like you!'

'The man of honour kills. But there's another sort who doesn't. The man of honour goes by what the priest, the judge and the rich man say, and under his cloak he always carries a knife. They are terrible, these men of honour, and they've always got public opinion, God and the Law on their side! The wretched and the lowly can stew in their own juice.'

He stopped speaking. Around him they drank and pronounced judgment. Some backed Louvadeus. Someone else said:

'If I were robbed of what I'd earned by my sweat, and I caught the thief, I'd feel like giving it to him too.'

Manuel went over to him, his glass half tumbled and spilling wine.

'So you'd kill him, eh? Look here! Killing a man is a very serious matter. Even if it's to avenge a wrong, it's always an evil that cries to the heavens. If you killed someone, lad, because they'd stolen your money, you'd be no better than the worst of murderers. A man's life is a marvellous thing: a mechanism that's so perfect nobody knows how to wind it up properly. There's nothing in the world to justify destroying it. Yes, indeed! To break it up before its time is a great sin before the sun, the stars, the mountains that look on us from far off, the insects, and the rooks that pass in the sky and can see.'

Everybody was struck dumb. This sounded too much like a sermon. Surely it wasn't necessary to understand everything?

Aquilino Ribeiro, When the Wolves Howl
translated by Patricia McGowanPinheiro

first court, but renovations have made it almost as characterless as the **Palace of the Dukes of Bragança** (open 10 am–5 pm, closed Tuesday) below. Built in 1401 by the first Duke, this palace was abandoned in favour of another at Vila Vicosa and left in ruins for centuries until given a tasteless overhaul in 1933. Thirty-nine brick chimneys are its most striking feature. The overpriced tour by an indifferent guide has little to recommend it other than the pleasure of seeing some Persian rugs and Aubusson tapestries, a Josefa de Óbidos painting of a lamb and unusual wood ceilings in the style of a caravel's hull. Between the castle and palace is the little **Church of São Miguel** where Afonso was baptized; in its simplicity it has more atmosphere than either massive monument.

The town's museums, however, are excellent. The **Museu de Alberto Sampaio** (open 10 am–12.30 pm, 2–5.30 pm, closed Monday) is housed in the conventual buildings of the Collegiate Church of N S da Oliveira, around a Romanesque cloister. The prize item is a gleaming silver triptych of the Nativity, believed to have come from the King of Castile's tent after the 1385 Battle of Aljubarrota. The tunic that João I wore in the battle is also displayed, among a weight of silver crosses, chalices, goblets and chests.

On the other side of town, the **Museu de Martins Sarmento** (open 10 am–noon, 2–5 pm, closed Monday) is chock-a-block with discoveries from the Celto-Iberian hillforts of Briteiros and Sabroso. Although the attentive guide likes to linger on various Roman remains, the most striking items are a curious bronze votive ox cart from Trás-os-Montes (fourth century BC); two headless Lusitanian granite soldiers clasping shields to their tummies; and the controversial 2,000-year-old *pedra formosa*, a huge slab of stone with a semi-circular bite from its base. Unlike the similar one at Briteiros, this *pedra* is believed to have served a funerary purpose. Most mysterious of all is the massive Henry Moore-like figure called the **Colossus of Pedralva**, towering over the surrounding stones with one arm outstretched. Someone made him perhaps 3,000 years ago, but who and why no-one knows.

Braga

The ancient Roman city of Bracara Augusta is best known for its dozens of churches and its religious aura. In recent times industry has made Braga, the capital of the Minho, as busy as its bishops once did, though the fervent celebrations during Easter Week reveal that it still savours its role as the nation's religious capital, seat of the powerful Primate of Portugal.

Everything centres around the cathedral, cheek-by-jowl with the Misericórdia church and Braga's main pedestrianized shopping street. Opposite is the fortress-style **Archbishop's Palace**, now used mainly by the university and public library (valuable city archives are kept in the Gothic keep).

The oldest parts of the originally Romanesque **cathedral** are the south and western doors (the latter, the 'main' doorway, facing Rua D Paio Mendes, is sheltered by a Gothic portico). But the most dramatic feature is the sixteenth-century pinnacled roofline by João de Castilho (later the architect of Belém's Jerónimos Monastery).

Getting your bearings inside the cathedral can be confusing; it is best to enter through the northern courtyard of chapels (opposite the Archbishop's Palace) and find the elderly guide clanking with keys to lead you from one dark chamber to another. The **King's Chapel** contains the tombs of the cathedral's founders—Henri of Burgundy and his wife Teresa—and the gruesome mummified remains of the fourteenth-century Archbishop Lourenço Vicente, who fought in the Battle of Aljubarrota. **St Gerald's Chapel** is covered with *azulejos* on the life of St Gerald (first archbishop of Braga), but the best of the trio is the **Chapel of Glory**, with cracked and fading fourteenth-century murals, and the finely sculptured tomb of Dom Gonçalo Pereira displaying a row of Apostles like choir boys, singing with mouths wide open.

Other memorable bits of the cathedral are its gilded *coro alto* with two giant baroque organs poised to blast each other, and the **Treasury museum,** in the midst of a long-overdue renovation at the time of writing. Its assorted contents include priceless but moth-eaten vestments, an iron cross used in Brazil's first mass in 1500, silver chalices, illuminated manuscripts, and even some fancy high-heeled shoes for the diminutive eighteenth-century Archbishop D. Rodrigo de Moura Teles who wielded tremendous power and influence despite not being able to reach the altar.

Braga has two of the most enjoyable **museums** in the country as well as two of its most tedious (the Pio XII and Medina). Save your energy for the **Casa dos Biscainhos Museum** (open 10 am–noon, 2–5 pm, closed Monday). This was the Nesfereira's family home from the 1760s until 1963 and still displays much of their lavish furnishings in rooms of pink walls and elaborate ceiling mouldings. Through the entrance lobby with its crisscross paving (to enable the carriages to draw right up to the foot of the stairway, an ingenious design for languorous nobility), you reach a rambling eighteenth-century garden with fountains, box hedges and bamboo groves overlooked by lichenous statues. Relocated Roman milestones bearing Caesar's and Nero's names look quite at home here.

The **Casa Nogueira da Silva Museum** (Avenida dos Combatentes, open 3–5 pm, closed Monday), is an eclectic private collection: elephant tusks in the chrome and glass hallway set the tone for the mix of Aubusson tapestries and silver chalices, sixteenth -century Flemish triptychs and twentieth-century Jorge Barradas busts with hairdos of blue fruits and flowers. In the main room, glass doors reveal an enchanting garden of half-hidden surprises: statues and *azulejo* panels, old stone fonts and rose arbours.

Among other pleasures in Braga are the **Fonte do Idolo**, a mystic little Roman sanctuary down some steps in Rua do Raio; and the **A Brasileiro** and **Viana cafés** on the central Praça da República, where you can mingle with the city's students, priests and entrepreneurs in surroundings of old-fashioned style.

Around Braga

The two most famous sights outside Braga are the Celto-Iberian hillfort of Briteiros and the baroque Bom Jesus do Monte with its monumental zigzag staircase. See **Bom Jesus** first, if only to recover from it at tranquil Briteiros.

Two kilometres (1.2 miles) east of Braga, Bom Jesus has been a popular pilgrimage site ever since its granite and white plaster stairway was completed in the 1780s, offering the perfect penance for devotees climbing the Holy Way on their knees. A funicular now provides a tempting alternative but only by walking will you be able to appreciate the allegorical fountains representing the five senses and three virtues, and the side chapels en route with their disturbingly realistic terracotta figures portraying the story of Christ. The woods at the top offer a pleasant stroll, with three more chapels, a café and lake.

The **Citânia de Briteiros** (open 9 am–7.30 pm) is the most spectacular of the Minho's many Celto-Iberian hillforts and believed to have been the last stronghold against the Romans. Excavated in the 1870s, it clearly shows the low stone circular walls of over 150 dwellings, as well as paths and water channels, wells and fonts. Two reconstructed huts with thatch roofs stand at the top of the hill, but most intriguing is what lies at the bottom: a long barrow of stone slabs, with an ornately carved portal. It looks like a tomb, but keep your imagination in check: the experts now reckon it was simply the baths.

Barcelos

Three things make Barcelos famous: its huge Thursday market, one of the best in the country; its brown, yellow-dotted pottery and weird ceramic figurines; and most obviously, its cockerel, symbol of tourist Portugal. It was here 600 years ago (so the legend goes) that a Galician pilgrim, accused of theft, successfully bet that a roasted cock on the judge's table would prove his innocence by standing up and crowing. The 'Gentleman of the Cock' stone cross in the town's **Archaeological Museum** (open 10 am–noon, 2–6 pm, closed Monday) nicely illustrates the legend.

Barcelos's morning **market** fills the central Campo da República with shoes and clothes and mounds of bread, squawking hens and quivering rabbits, baskets, hats and wine barrels, bellows and belts and grates. Patient women in black stand over their piles of onions and sprigs of parsley; potters spread their wares into the sunshine and buxom clothes-sellers in long skirts and dangling earrings holler prices, their children curled up among heaps of bras and corsets.

At lunchtime they all descend on the **Pensão Bagoeira** (57 Avenida Dr Sidónio Pais) for soup and take-away roast veal buns, or a sit-down family splurge of *rōjoes à moda do minho* (fried pork nuggets), wine and strawberries.

Throughout the morning, market-goers slip into the imposing eighteenth-century **Church of Nosso Senhor da Cruz** to kneel on the stone floor before gilt chapels and walls of star-studded *azulejos*; others put their fresh lilies on the altar in the **Church of Our Lady of Terço**, and whisper confessions among *azulejos* by the master tile-maker, Antonio de Oliveira Bernardes. He added some awesome touches to disturb their thoughts—a dancing half-goat, half-devil, a many-headed winged beast, and most awful of all for a Barcelos man, a devilish cockerel preening himself in a mirror.

The Peneda-Gerês National Park

Curving around the crook-shaped Spanish border, this huge national park (at 72,000 hectares or 280 square miles the largest reserve in Portugal) encompasses over a hundred villages in its granite mountain ranges (the Peneda and Gerês) as well as a clutch of major reservoirs. Caldas do Gerês, the main centre, gets crowded on holidays, but you can easily find remoter spots. The maps available from the park's office in Gerês are close to useless, so serious walkers should try and get a Portuguese friend to buy a military map (not sold to foreigners) at Oporto's Porto Editoria (Rua da Fabrica); these military maps pre-date the dams and reservoirs but are the best available.

Caldas do Gerês is a charming old spa town with plenty of accommodation, everything from old-fashioned hotels on the main street to upstart pensions above the wooded gorge. The elderly and infirm sit in the arcade by the spa's hospital playing cards, or in front of the hotels' televisions, diligently knitting. Nights here are very quiet.

A popular excursion up to the 836-metre (2,541-foot) high **Pedra Bela** viewpoint, seven kilometres (4.3 miles) east of Gerês, gives a spectacular panorama over the surrounding hills and Caniçada dam. From here a downhill track offers a lovely walk through the ferns and firs to Ermida village (six kilometres or 3.7 miles) where you can find simple overnight accommodation.

A more intriguing route starts just before the border of **Portela do Homem**, 12 kilometres (seven miles) north of Gerês. Take the track to the left marked 'Campo' (eight kilometres or five miles): this is part of the Roman road that once linked Braga to Astorga in Spain, and it is still studded with Roman milestones. Through the silent forest and from the hillsides further on you catch increasingly dramatic views of the reservoir of Vilharino das Furnas. A sense of wilderness is only lost at Campo itself, where you will find a café and buses back to Gerês.

The Costa Verde

The rainy, rough 'green coast' of the Minho may not have the best swimming, but it does have some fine seaside towns, not least **Viana do Castelo,** famous for its carnival *romaria* in August. This once-unrivalled fishing port on the Lima estuary, backed by the wooded Monte de Santa Luzia, has none of the tackiness of a beach resort—perhaps because its best beach, the **Praia do Cabedelo**, lies some distance away, across the river. In town, attention is centred around the

impressive **Praça da República** with its Renaissance fountain, restored town hall, and curious Misericórdia House, its sixteenth-century three-tiered façade borne by asexual, flat-breasted caryatids.

Another popular fountain—the soppy Statue of Viana in the Jardim Marginal—is a favourite photographer's spot, where statue, town hall and hilltop **Church of Santa Luzia** are all visible in a row. A funicular climbs the hill every hour from 10 am to 6 pm, but the walk through pine forests is better: cross the railway track and follow steps beside the large white Misericórdia building. The neo-Byzantine basilica itself is an ugly blot but the view out to sea from here is great.

Among Viana's fine mansions, the former eighteenth-century palace of the Barbosa Macieis family provides an appropriate setting for the **Municipal Museum** (open 9.30 am–12.30 pm, 2–5 pm, closed Monday), its walls upstairs covered with whimsical *azulejos* of the continents by Policarpo de Oliveira Bernardes. The museum's collection is rich in seventeenth-and eighteenth-century ceramics and ivory-inlaid Indo-Portuguese furniture. Look out for two unusual pieces: an altar hidden within a carved teak chest, and a painting of a black magic ritual.

The Minho Valley

Caminha, on the River Minho frontier, is full of character, its central square featuring a Viana-style fountain and crusty old houses. Souvenir shops selling linen and local copperware are geared to Spanish day-trippers. But walk under the arch of the Renaissance clock tower (once part of fourteenth-century fortifications) and you will come to the **Igreja Matriz** (parish church), a fifteenth-century fortress-church renowned for its ceiling of carved maplewood in Moorish style (if it is closed ask for the key at the Turismo office in the same lane). The Renaissance doorway features a naked man, bending to point his bum at Spain.

Through **Vila Nova de Cerveira** with its *pousada* fortress and regular ferry crossings to Spain, you reach the Minho's most imposing fortified town, **Valença do Minho**, whose fortress-within-a-fortress has stared at the Galician town of Tuy across the river for over 300 years. It is now a convenient self-enclosed shopping centre for Spanish visitors (the modern town below caters for everything else), each shop housed in a stylish mansion with wrought-iron balconies. At dusk, when the day-trippers have gone, a solitary air creeps up on Valença from the riverside banks below, sliding over its mossy turrets, its bastions, cannons and ramparts, and into the abandoned cobbled streets.

But for atmosphere day and night, the quiet little town of **Monção** has the edge on Valença. Off the chestnut-shaded Praça da República ancient lanes lead to all kinds of local lore. One takes you under an arch to the **Igreja Matriz** and its cenotaph to Deu-la-Deu, a local heroine who saved the starving townsfolk from Castilians in 1368. She scraped together enough flour to make two buns which she nonchalantly offered the enemy, and this apparent evidence of plentiful supplies so disheartened them that they gave up the siege and left.

Another lane leads into Rua de Indepencia where you will find a real den of a *tasca* (tavern) and one of the old city gates. The river ambience below has been ruined by a quarry on the Spanish side, but it is still a pleasant walk to the nearby riverside spa. Tourists are unexpected visitors but the cheery staff will welcome you for a 15-minute thermal bath (Es.190), an *irrigaçoes* treatment or *pulverizaçoes*.

The most dramatic stretch of the Minho is between Monção and Melgaço, with the mountains slowly closing in on the river, bringing hills of vines and granite villages, a roadside of roses and blue rhododendrons. **Melgaço** itself is quaint, tucking an old fortress keep amongst flower-filled alleys. Delve into the wooded hills near the town to discover all kinds of surprises, such as the solitary Romanesque **Paderne Church**, three kilometres (two miles) up from Peso, with beautifully carved doors of petals and roses.

The Lima Valley

The route from Monção south to the River Lima is one of the most enchanting in the Minho province, passing the lonely panoramic heights at **Extremo**

Castanheira and a squat Roman bridge at **Rubiães**. In between is **Paredes de Coura** which was once on the Roman Braga to Astorga road. Now it is a convenient walking base with Swiss vistas of neatly-cultivated hillsides and pockets of old, traditional life. **Santa** hamlet, a 15-minute walk from town, has a water-powered flour mill beside an old carpenter's shed.

The Romans thought the Lima was too good to be true: believing it to be the Lethe, the River of Oblivion, Decimus Junius Brutus' troops refused to cross it until he himself had seized the standard and plunged ahead, shouting the names of his legionaries from the far side.

Now there is nothing nicer than to cross the Lima by the Roman bridge at **Ponte de Lima**, a dreamy town that trails along a broad sandy riverbank behind rows of plane trees. A couple of riverside pensions make it easy to linger, though you might like to investigate nearby **Turismo de Habitação** (manor house) accommodation (see page 176) as the central booking office is based here, in the Turismo office.

Sightseeing in Ponte de Lima is very low-key. The multi-padlocked keep (the only bit left of the town's fortifications) has only an arts and crafts shop; in a lane behind is the **Igreja Matriz** with grapes and cherubs climbing up a side altar. Meanwhile, downriver, a boozy custodian gives a rambling tour of the former Convent of São Antonio and adjacent Church of São Francisco, now housing the **Museu des Terceiros** (open 10 am–noon, 2–6 pm, closed Tuesday; ring the bell and wait for the guide to emerge from the depths of the convent). Assorted folklore items, medieval *azulejos*, and a vestment chest are climaxed by the church of São Francisco itself with its elaborately gilt altars and pulpits.

But riverside meanders are the best of all for spotting the local specialities— stone *alminhas* ('little souls'—shrines) and *cruzeiros* (crosses). At dusk, boys gallop their horses across the bridge, and you are nudged into another world.

Those hooked on Lima magic can pause again at **Ponte de Barca** whose tiny old town has the same air of drowsy content and a similarly-styled arched bridge. Swimming in the river here has the advantage of deeper water and shadier spots.

Parts of the old town are very ramshackle, with derelict doorways and crumbling window sills. The arcaded seventeenth-century market in the neat garden by the bridge provides an incongruous formal touch.

While in this area, go to the roadside hamlet of **Bravães**, (six kilometres or 3.7 miles west) which has one of the finest Romanesque churches in Portugal, with intricately carved doorways of griffin and sheep, doves and monkeys.

Just north of Ponte de Barca is **Arcos de Valdevez,** which curls around the River Vez, a tributary of the Lima. The steep little town overlooks an older quarter, linked to it by an eighteenth-century bridge. A park with willowy banks attracts fishermen and lovers. It is pleasant for a visit, but Ponte de Barca makes a better stopover, if only for motherly Maria Gomes and her riverside *pensão* with its tiny attic rooms and shining wooden floors.

Off the Track

East of Ponte de Barca, in the Peneda-Gerês Park, are some of the wildest areas of the Minho, with rough, tough mountain villages like Soajo and Lindoso. **Soajo** on market day is a treat, with stalls of scissors, cowbells, pots and pans, rat traps, clogs and wine barrels. In the central square, with its strange pillory carved with a smiling sun's face, men and women haggle over livestock while horses are shoed near the church, the neighing and mooing quietly merging with the sound of mass.

A few minutes' walk from the square are dozens of *espigueiros* (stone granaries raised up on mushroom-shaped stones), a common Minho method for drying and storing maize. With their stone crosses (symbolizing the sacredness of maize) and long, cold chambers, they look disturbingly like coffins.

Even more famous for its *espigueiros* is nearby **Lindoso.** From Soajo the road winds steeply down into the Lima valley and up again past a hydroelectric dam to the hilltop village. Its ancient castle (see the huge bread oven inside), just a few kilometres from the Spanish border, has faced many attacks; now it offers peaceful views of the *espigueiros* huddled below.

Past the church, a cobbled path covered with vine trellises leads up into the lonely hills beyond. Among the village's newer *casas de emigrante* are older, more secretive shelters, carved from the mountain's rock and stone. Given the chance, you could burrow down here very peacefully from the world.

Another haven is surprisingly close to Braga city: the tiny Visigothic chapel of **São Frutuoso de Montélios** (open 10.30 am–noon, 2–4 pm, until 6.30 pm in summer, closed Monday), built on a Greek cross plan, destroyed by the Moors and restored in the eleventh century. Tucked off the main road, it preserves its curious individuality, despite adjoining an eighteenth-century church.

Follow the N201 300 metres (330 yards) further, turn left and left again to reach the **Monastery of Tibães** (open 9 am–noon, 2–7 pm, closed Monday). Once the grandest Benedictine monastery in Portugal, owning vast estates, linen mills, farms and craft enterprises, it fell into ruin after the 1834 dissolution of religions and is only now being restored: different quarters are gradually being converted into a *pousada*, museum and baroque art school.

While they last, Tibães' ruins and gardens are dense with atmosphere. The cloister and vast kitchens are covered in weeds, and a stairway with carved stone fonts zigzags up the overgrown hillside (its design, some say, later inspired the famous stairway of Bom Jesus). The huge Chapter House has walls of exquisite eighteenth-century *azulejos* over a floor of rotten planks. Best preserved is the church where you can see how the monastery flaunted its seventeenth-century wealth in a baroque organ, rococo altar and a mass of gilt woodcarving. The adventurous choir stalls are carved with grimacing faces and animals ranging from elephants to lions; with such extensive grounds, perhaps the canny monk-entrepreneurs envisaged a baroque safari park.

Variation on a Theme

All the barbarity and blood that a bullfight in Spain involves was done away with here when, under D. Pedro, so many changes for the better we brought about. The bull's horns are bandaged so that they cannot kill the wretched horses.

The amphitheatre is an enormous square building with three tiers of boxes, all under cover. The arena, on the other hand, is octagonal and open. They were mostly ordinary folk, farmers and fishermen, whom I saw gathered there. The boxes were completely filled and presented a very motley sight. The band played Spanish boleros and then a young man rode in, got up in party clothes and much coiffured; he bowed to all sides. The bull was sent in and it was not long before it had a dart in the side of its neck. Two young farmers also took part in the fight, and showed themselves to be well practised bandarilheiros. They were handsome men, dressed in velvet and gold-braid, their hair set as if they were going to a ball. In addition to these there were three other older bandarlheiros and some peasants in white trousers and coloured jackets patterned with large flowers. Here, as in Spain, at the end of the fight the barriers were opened and a herd of tame bulls, with bells round their necks, were let in to round up the fighting bulls, who left the arena, roaring and dripping with blood from the many darts that had pierced the skin of their necks. A feature that I had not seen in Spain, was that the farmers, who had brought the bulls in from the country, also showed their skill. They stationed themselves in front of the door to the pen or lay down on the ground outside, inviting an attack from the bull, but by a quick spring into the air and a sharp twist they showed how to avoid the blow and to place themselves between the horns of the animal, which then ran some distance with them, to the general rejoicing of the crowd.

Hans Christian Andersen, A Visit to Portugal, *1866*

Trás-os-Montes

Portugal's northeast province is one of the rarest corners of Europe. Its name, 'behind-the-mountains', refers to more than the geographical shield of the Marão and Gerês ranges: it implies a Tolkien mystery found in isolated villages of shale, and lingering pagan cults. Urban Portuguese are in the habit of warning you away from the place: 'It's very backward,' they murmur. 'Roads are poor, accommodation bad. It's a hundred, 300 years behind.'

Still, some of the most memorable pockets of Portugal are found in these high plateaux and rugged valleys, with their dramatic extremes of temperature. And it is not all so remote: even in the farthest corner—Bragança—a highway from Oporto is edging closer, to connect with Zamora in Spain. The Chaves–Bragança–Tua circuit is admittedly still a long drive but the Tua to Bragança narrow-gauge railway provides a convenient alternative as well as being one of the greatest train rides in Portugal.

Off the track (actually, for most tourists, all of Trás-os-Montes will be off the beaten track) there are sights and experiences to shake your view of life: inexplicable stone carvings and pagan rituals; balancing boulders and weird mask dances; or simply, perhaps, a glimpse into a villager's simple granite home—chickens in the kitchen, pigs grunting in the barn below.

Lucky is the traveller who goes beyond the mountains with time and an open mind, for he or she will find experiences usually granted only in their dreams.

Vila Real

The dramatic road over the Marão mountains is a hard act to follow; Vila Real's sprawling industrial town (the largest in the province) cannot possibly compete, unless you are interested in motorcycling (international races are held here in June and July), or construction work ('bursting everywhere,' trumpets the Turismo brochure, 'in a non-stopping rhythm').

The real reason to stop here lies some three kilometres (a couple of miles) to the southeast: **Solar de Mateus** (open 9 am–12.30 pm, 2–5 pm), the baroque country house made famous on the label of Mateus Rosé wine. The first thing that catches your eye is not the famed facade (now half-hidden by a huge tree), nor, as seen on the bottles, the lake's gliding swan (it does not have one), but a modern sculpture by João Cutileiro of a half-submerged naked lady at the lake's edge. Once over this shock you look at the palace with new eyes.

English poet and critic Sacheverell Sitwell described it as 'the most fantastic country house in Portugal'. Created by Nicolau Nasoni in the 1740s, the granite and white-washed wings of the house ('advancing lobster-like towards you', wrote Sitwell) shelter a cobbled forecourt dominated by a balustraded stairway, rooftop spires and statues. Feast your eyes, for the expensive entrance ticket includes a tour of just a few rooms, heavy with velvet drapes and fussy eighteenth-century furnishings. The small family museum is best, with fans, dolls, medals and pistols as well as a rare first modern edition (1817) of *The Lusiads* with three of the original copperplate engravings by Fragonard and Baron Gerard.

The formal gardens behind the palace are like a scene from Alice in Wonderland: tiny box hedges, prim little statues, and best of all, a perfectly moulded tunnel of trees, very dark and fragrant, with pools of sunshine at either end. As for the Mateus Rosé wine, it is no longer made here but by Sogrape down the road; at the ticket lodge you can buy the palace's own select brew instead, or Mateus jams of pumpkin, plum or peach.

Chaves

Vila Real used to be famous for another quaint delight: the Corgo Line's narrow-gauge railway north to Chaves. This much-loved line has now been axed, and the service replaced by buses. Eventually a major highway is planned to link the region with the other end of the country.

But Chaves still has an end-of-the-line feel; the last stop, as it were, before the wilder areas of Trás-os-Montes. Historically, it has always been a first stop for invaders into Portugal: the Spanish border is just ten kilometres (five-and-a-half miles) away. French, Spanish, Moors, Romans, Suevi and Visigoths have all squabbled over strategic Chaves (significantly translating as 'keys'), although the Romans at least made the spa famous and left a useful bridge. Aquae Flaviae, as they called the town, was a major stop on the Braga to Astorga road. Latin scholars can read all about it from milestones still standing on the bridge.

The historical core of Chaves is around Praça de Camões, off the picturesque Rua Direita with its old wood-balcony houses. The massive fourteenth-century keep behind the Praça is all that remains of the castle where the first Duke of Bragança once lived. It is now a **military museum** surrounded by attractive gardens; but the adjacent **Museu de Regiao Flaviense** (open 9.30 am–12.30 pm, 2–5 pm, closed Monday and weekend mornings) is more worthwhile, with its prehistoric remains (one jar, with geometric patterns, is dated 2700 BC), stone carvings, phallic menhirs and folk crafts.

In the Praça itself, peep inside the **Misericórdia** to see the darkly painted ceiling and imaginative eighteenth-century *azulejos* depicting the life of Christ. The **Igreja Matriz** has a dramatic organ, supported by huge bearded heads.

The Rua Santa Maria behind the Igreja leads to Chaves' self-proclaimed best *tipico* restaurant and cake shop, O Antigo Pasteleiro, with delicious meat pasties, a Chaves speciality. Other local goodies are smoked ham (*presunto*) honey and black pottery. On the drinks side, you are unlikely to rave about the warm, alkaline spa waters (free doses down by the riverside spa hospital) but it may do wonders for your metabolic disorders, diabetes, gout or obesity.

If not, head for **Vidgao**, 17 kilometres (nine miles) southwest, whose waters are equally popular. The slim and healthy get distracted by Vidago's peach-pink Edwardian **Palace Hotel**, with its leather armchairs and sweeping staircase.

Last-ditch liquid cures may be found at nearby **Boticas**, an unremarkable place that produces the remarkable *vinho dos mortos,* 'Wine of the Dead'. It all began in 1809 when villagers buried their wine to conceal it from the invading French. Discovering afterwards that the taste had improved, they have carried on burying bottles ever since, usually for a year or two. There are only a couple of places in town where you can find the stuff—at the Restaurante Santa Cruz, or the bus-stop Café de Armindo (9 Rua de Sangunhedo) whose barman will recommend an accompanying meat pasty to complement (disguise?) the wine's gritty flavour.

The Barroso Villages: Back in Time

In the area west of Chaves, around the huge **Barragem do Alto Rabagão** lake, are tiny, self-sufficient villages in the folds of the Serra do Barroso and the Serra do Larouca. Here is Trás-os-Montes lifestyle at its toughest and truest: for most villagers, it is a hard life of little reward, with a poor soil to till, bitter winters to endure and only the return of emigrant sons and their wealth to look forward to.

Vilarino Sêco, at the lonely end of the road from Alturas do Barroso, is typical: cobbled streets caked with dung, houses made of huge granite blocks, pigs grunting from behind wood doors. A few kids flick sticks, bored. Cockcrow and cowbells alternate with the dripping water of the village font to fill the silence. At dusk, the women bring in goats, and large, healthy cows: 'at least the pasture's good here,' says one, wrapping her woollens closer around her, 'but life in France is better.'

On the other side of the lake, hilltop **Montalegre** is the largest town in the area, flush with emigrant money (the modern square sports a new statue entitled *Ao Emigrante*). The remains of a four-towered, fourteenth-century castle are of minimal interest to archaeologists who have found the surrounding area richer, full of prehistoric remnants. But to those undefended villages like nearby Sendim, right on the Spanish border, the distant castle is still reassuring. Surrounded by rolling hills of broom, **Sendim** smells of its animals: donkeys in the doorways, hens in the road, cows in the fields.

Neighbouring **Pardornelos** is more affluent, with new additions to its old stone cottages. A Spanish-looking lady on her donkey stops to talk. 'I've been hoeing! Are you hungry? Come and eat!' She smacks her lips in unmistakeable mime, clicks her donkey onwards and leads me home. Out go the hens from the smoke-blackened kitchen, in comes a plate of *presunto*, a loaf of bread—'eat, eat!'—and a jug of wine—'drink!' Angelina's husband was ill in hospital, her son in France. Life, she said, was hard.

At **Seara Velha** I watched Manuel Dacruze unhitch his oxen from the cart.
'Will you take a glass of wine?' he asked, and opened up the barn to get a bottle.
'Down it in one!' laughed his wife. *'Nao faz mal!* Never mind, it's not strong!'
Every villager here speaks French, recalling years of money-earning toil in
Lyons, Paris or Bordeaux. 'All the young men leave for France,' said the café-
owner. 'There used to be so many children, now there are so few. It's sad. Our
village is healthy, quiet, and beautiful. But there's nothing for the young. And
life is very hard, very hard. . .'

Bragança

Stones are often special in Trás-os-Montes. And none more so than the **Pedra
de Bolideira,** 16 kilometres (nine miles) east of Chaves just off the Bragança
road (turn left at Bolideira along a track signposted 'Travancas'). This huge,
boulder sliced in two is beached like a whale on a grassy mound, its lower half
balanced and rockable. Picnicking under its shade requires steady nerves.

Arriving at Bragança after a stretch of dreamy landscape, the ugly outskirts
and highway construction work come as a shock. But take the road up to the
pousada de São Bartolomeu and the best face of this remote capital of the
province reveals itself. Its old walled citadel is set on a hill above the new town
and is a striking symbol of Bragança— and Portuguese—independence. It was
the eighth Duke of Bragança who ousted Philip II of Spain from the throne in
1640, beginning a Bragança dynasty of kings that lasted until 1910.

Not that the royal family influenced Bragança much. They spent most of
their time down south, in their Vila Viçosa palace. So Bragança has no preten-
sions: it is a market and university town, an agricultural centre, used to making
its own decisions.

Within the twelfth-century **citadel** there is a cluster of white-washed cottages. Despite a few souvenir shops you get the impression nothing has changed
much over the centuries: the old women still sit on their doorsteps, crocheting,
the cats leap across the rooftops, the hens scrabble in the lanes. The Gothic
keep, however, is now a **Military Museum** (open 9 am–12.30 pm, 2–5 pm,
closed Thursday) with spears and suits of armour and a rooftop view of the
endless surrounding hills that make you appreciate Bragança's utter isolation.

Beside the castle, and the dull **Church of Santa Maria**, is the twelfth-
century **Domus Municipalis**, the oldest meeting hall in Portugal, with an
intriguing pentagonal design and stone-carved faces of men and beasts. The
pillory, in the shadow of the keep, is another oddity, piercing a prehistoric
granite pig. There are hundreds of these mysterious stone animals (called
berrões) scattered throughout Trás-os-Montes; benign-looking fellows, they are
believed to have been idols or offerings to the gods.

Pigs are still a firm favourite in the region (try the *feijoada à Transmontana*
for the most piggish of stews). In Bragança's **market** (just off the central Largo

da Sé) the stalls are full of smoked sausages and hams, including a modern version of the *alheira* sausages that were originally made by sixteenth-century Jews to convince the Inquisition they were eating pork (the sausages were actually made of turkey). If you follow Rua Dr Paul Teixera to the left behind the market you will reach the old **Jewish quarter** of Rua dos Fornos, a secluded corner of town with cottages clustered together beside the River Fervença.

Near the main **Turismo** office the **Church of São Vicente** is where Dom Pedro claimed to have married his Spanish lover, Inês de Castro. It is notable now for a bizarre three-D figure of Christ leaping down from the ceiling, with four other figures ready to follow. Artistically, though, the Renaissance **Church of São Bento** is the winner in town, with a *trompe l'oeil* ceiling of burnished blues and golds and a contrasting Mudéjar-style ceiling in the chancel.

On the same Rua Abilio Beça is the **Museu do Abade de Baçal** (open 10 am–12.30 pm, 2–5 pm, closed Monday), housed in the former bishop's palace. Its curiosities and treasures include sacred art and silverware, costumes, cauldrons and door-knockers, as well as a nasty-looking medieval 'scold's bridle'. The box-hedged garden outside is dotted with Roman funerary stones, prehistoric granite pigs and odd little stone figures with arms to their ankles.

Around Bragança

Difficult to find among the highway construction, the remains of the twelfth-century church of the Benedictine **Monastery of Castro de Avelãs** is in a village a few kilometres west of Bragança, and now incorporated into the parish church. Built of brick with blind arcades (the only one of its kind in Portugal), one part of its triple apse stands forlornly in the open. Two stone lions (one headless, the other with bared teeth) once topped the gate; now they lie for safety on the ground, in a soft bed of poppies.

Bragança is a perfect base for exploring the **Parque Natural de Montezinho**, the hilly northeastern knuckle of Portugal. One route to the border village of **Portelo** takes you along the green Sabor valley, with shaggy chestnuts by the road and a jungle of birdsong; beehives and horseshoe-shaped pigeon coops (a unique feature of the region) are scattered on the flowery meadows behind **Franca**.

Another route leads to the curious border village of **Rio de Onor**. Its Spanish neighbour (with the same name) is separated by a chain slung across the path between stone blocks marked 'E' and 'P'. Locals take no notice of it (a dozy Pekingese is the only watchdog on the Spanish side). They even speak a mixed dialect, called Rionorês. The village itself reflects the toughness of their remote lives: straw stacked under slate stairways, firewood in the shed and cottages of cold, grey stone.

Miranda do Douro

Within spitting distance from the awesome Douro gorge that marks the frontier with Spain, Miranda do Douro has notched up a succession of inevitable border battles. The climax was a Franco-Spanish attack in 1762 which destroyed most of its castle. Like Valença on the River Minho border, its old walled citadel now welcomes Spanish day-trippers who come to buy cheap Portuguese linen; also like Valença, an ugly new town is developing outside the walls.

But old Miranda is still beguiling. Its wide cobbled streets are bordered by imposing houses, some bearing stone crests. Little is left of the sixteenth-century Bishop's Palace except an arch, but the former **cathedral** reveals Miranda's moment of glory: the Pope unexpectedly created a diocese in Miranda in 1545 so a cathedral was built to grand scale, with gilded altarpieces and choir stalls, painted arches, and a fantastic organ, supported by a suitably dour, devil-deflecting face.

The diocese was transferred to Bragança in the eighteenth-century, provoking the local rebuke, 'the sacristy is in Bragança, but the cathedral is in Miranda.' Affections are now centred on a rosy-cheeked porcelain boy Jesus in a glass case in the south transept. Created in the last century, he has been given a wardrobe of seventeenth-century-style silk brocade suits and top hats (his favourite headgear).

But the best place in Miranda for discovering quaint customs is the

Museu da Terra de Miranda, which has everything from crude agricultural implements to a 'typical' Mirandês-style bedroom and kitchen. The 'Sunday best' outfits on display indicate the rigours of a local winter, with garments beautifully made in thick wool and felt. A shaggy straw coat used to be the shepherd's best protection against the cold and rain.

There are some weird costumes for festivals: in Vila-Cha, a man in woman's dress carries an inflated pig's bladder, stick and crook to persuade villagers to part with their money at New Year for a pig feast. More elaborate are the costumes of the famous *pauliteiros*, or 'stick-dancers' (the sticks were probably once swords).

This bizarre fertility dance, perhaps dating back to the first century, is still performed by a local team from Duas Igrejas, whose eight members range in age from 14 to 74. 'But it's getting much harder to attract young dancers these days,' says the team's director, 73-year-old Antonio Maria Mourinho, who has led them for 50 years. 'The young don't understand our thoughts. They're only interested in football, alcohol and sex.' Your best chance of catching the **pauliteiros de Miranda** before those other potent forces have their way is at the Festas de Santa Bárbara on the third Sunday in August.

Freixo de Espada-à-Cinta

Freixo is the end of Portugal, both spiritually and practically. Surrounded by wild, heathery hills where hawks and black kites soar, Freixo encapsulates that 'beyond-the-mountain' feeling. In early spring, thousands of blossoming almond trees lure Spaniards across the border, just three kilometres (two miles miles) east. For the rest of the year, Freixo is left alone. There is so little traffic that dogs sleep on the road.

It was not always so. Dom Afonso Henriques recognized Freixo's strategic importance over 800 years ago, and made the town a sanctuary for fugitives (excluding traitors) to promote its settlement. A century later, Dom Dinis felt secure enough to take a nap here (so the story goes), hanging his sword in an ash tree—hence the exotic town name, which means 'ash tree of the girth-sword'. In his waking hours he rebuilt the town's defences, adding the strange heptagonal **Cockerel's Tower** which still pinpoints the town for miles around.

The pride of Freixo is the sixteenth-century **Igreja Matriz** (parish church) below. Locals boast that the interior is like Belém's Jerónimos Monastery. It is certainly in the same style, with three naves of elaborate vaulting. Notable, too, is the retable of 16 panels ascribed to the famous sixteenth-century painter, Grão Vasco.

The town's unmarked **Museum** is the arched building on the right just before the church. But before you step inside, follow Rua Sacadura Cabral beside it until you reach Largo de Outeiro (look for Pensão Paris). In house no. 6 is

Freixo's least-advertised, most interesting attraction: **Casa de Bicho da Seda**—the house of silkworms. Here, about 25 women run Freixo's oldest industry, growing mulberry bushes in the back yard, and feeding the leaves to silkworms spread out on trays in the old house. One of the women will happily guide you round; listen to the steady chomping sound of a million feasting worms.

Back at the museum an old woman in black sits in the shadows spinning the cocoon fibres into silk thread while upstairs half-a-dozen women at looms weave them into cotton or linen-backed items. Both here and in the Casa de Bicho the finished products are for sale; if the prices hurt, there are cotton, crochet and lace alternatives.

By Train from Tua to Mirandela

Now that the authorities have axed Portugal's finest narrow-gauge train ride (the Corgo Line from Vila Real to Chaves) there is only one classic left: the **Tua Line** from Tua to Bragança. In all, it takes just under five hours, but the one-and-a-half-hour hop to Mirandela is an appealing taster.

The three-carriage train clatters slowly up from the Douro valley into the deep ravine of the Tua River where bony boulders are slotted in neat piles like vertebrae. Little white-washed stations appear from nowhere; villagers clamber on board to join ruddy-faced men, and women carrying baskets of cakes. Eucalyptus, olives and vines trail beside the track and the fig trees grow so close you can reach out and pluck the fruit. A man and his mule wait for the train to pass, shepherds look up, mesmerized still by the train's comings and goings.

At **Mirandela**, notable only for a long bridge built by the Romans, there is nothing better to do than come back by train to Tua or carry on to Bragança. But be warned: services on the Tua Line are now down to three a day (two only on weekends). Go before it is too late to experience the thrill of a slow arrival in the land beyond the mountains.

Off the Track

In terms of atmosphere, the prehistoric boulder of **Outeiro Machado** is stranger and more remote than almost anything else in Portugal. Just before the village of **Soutelo**, four kilometres (two-and-a-half miles) northwest of Chaves, follow a sign to 'Outeiro Machado' on the right. Take the left fork of this track past some new houses, turn right among the fir trees and fork left again until you reach an open sandy area. The huge boulder lies amongst ferns and heather to the right. Crawl all over it and you will find engravings, hieroglyphics, crosses and commas. What do they all mean? No-one knows.

Polite Society

We conversed at length, mainly about Lisbon, about our mutual friends, about the previous winter's parties and about the likelihood of future prospects.

We made disparaging remarks about Portuguese society and praised Paris and London to the skies, probably Peking and Nanking too, and came to the conclusion that even Timbuktu would be better than our wretched country's boring capital. Even so we missed it and, with a few concessions here and there, we eventually decided it wasn't such a bad place after all.

Admirable condition of human nature, that everything seems better and less ugly to us when seen from a distance!

The dullest public ball, with its hateful noise and confusion, where, in order to set eyes on a pleasant, familiar face, one had to weave a way through hundreds of barbarous elbows coming at one from all sides; to be trodden on cruelly by novice dancers, by some newly arrived member of parliament and by the editor of the Galocha's new boots and—worst of all!—to see the absurd toilettes, the fabulous hair-styles, the unbelievable faces and antediluvian figures of so many ugly and ungainly women. . . well, that same ball, when it is no longer more than a memory recollected in the boring surroundings of some tedious provincial town, seems quite different. The lights, the flowers, the music, all the bustle, are recalled with pleasure, while the rest is forgotten and a poor fellow involuntarily finds himself sighing for it.

The most boring soirée, with obligatory piano, sisters' duet, cousins' polka and elderly aunts playing cassino, recollected in the selfsame circumstances, also comes to be remembered as nothing other than a select, intimate gathering, with easy, pleasant conversation. . . oh, society's real pleasures!

As for the theatre, one has but to remember, when in the provinces, the sufferings his ear went through with the prima donna's bawlings, the tenor's cacophonies or the infuriating snores of that sleepy São Carlos orchestra!

The revolting translation of a comedy, riddled with incurable syphilis, at the Rua dos Condes theatre, is softened in the imagination by all the charm of Scribe's style.

And the frenzy of the original of an ultra–romantic drama, crowned with the unfading laurels of the Conservatory, for the eternal gaping of our mouths! At a distance, one applauds it enthusiastically, forgetting that one smoked outside during the whole of the first act, slept all through the second and chatted during the rest, until the unfailing scene with the ballad, the underground passage, the cemetery, or what have you, in which the lady, her hair dishevelled and dressed in a white gown, goes mad in style, the beau, drawing his hand across his forehead, wrenches from deep down in his thorax the compulsory three ahs! and swears he will kill his own father should he appear, the support player loses his support, whiskers tears out his whiskers . . . and damnation, hell and damnation!. . .'Ah, shameful woman! You know not that in this bosom beats a heart, that from this heart come arteries, from these arteries my veins—and in these veins runs blood . . . blood, blood! I want blood, because I thirst for something and that thing is blood . . . Ah! So you thought. . . Kneel, woman, I want to kill you . . . carve you in pieces, massacre you!' And the women kneels and there's nothing for it but to applaud. . .

And we always applaud.

I am not speaking for myself, because I like this sort of thing. What I'm getting at is that in the provinces there is none of this monotony, that one forgets the boring part and that from there one is not even aware of the sublime galimatias of the ridiculous.

Almeida Garrett, Travels in my Homeland
translated from the Portuguese by John M Parker

Festivals

Festivals are fantastic events in Portugal, featuring everything from religious processions and pilgrimages to folk songs and dances, fireworks and floral displays and sometimes even bullfights. During the summer, particularly in the northwest, a fair *(feira)* or religious festival in honour of a patron saint *(romaria)* held practically every weekend is your best chance of seeing the local costumes and traditions. The following lists some of the more spectacular festivals, but for exact dates and full details, ask the tourist board for their current festival booklet.

late February:	**Loulé, Algarve** Carnival—flowers and dances.
late February:	**Nazaré, Estremadura** Carnival—masked processions.
mid-March:	**Ovar, Beira Litoral** Procession—Franciscan monks and life-sized eighteenth-century images.
mid-March:	**Aveiro, Beira Litoral** Funfair—folk music and dancing.
Holy Week:	**Braga, Minho** Ceremonies and famous *Ecce Homo* processions.
Easter Sunday:	**Loulé, Algarve** Procession of devotees.
mid-April:	**Idanha-à-Nova, Beira Baixa** Folk Pilgrimage—songs and dances.
1 May:	**Alté, Algarve** Festival of folk songs and dances
3 May:	**Barcelos, Minho** Festival of Crosses—craft fairs and firework displays.
1st Sunday in May:	**Monsanto, Beira Baixa** Festival of the Castle (commemorating a legendary siege)—curious dances and rituals.

early May:	**Vila Franca do Lima, Minho** Festival of Our Lady of the Roses—beautiful procession of women carrying monumental baskets of rose petals on their heads.
12–13 May:	**Fátima, Ribatejo** lst Annual Pilgrimage commemorating the first apparition of the Virgin in 1917—hundreds of thousands of pilgrims arrive from all over Portugal.
lst weekend in June:	**Amarante, Douro** St Gonsalo Festival (ancient fertility cult)— fair, folk songs and dances.
lst fortnight in June:	**Santarém, Ribatejo** National Agricultural Fair—bullfights, folk songs and dances.
10–13 June:	**Amares and Vila Verde, Minho** St Anthony Festival—parades, folk songs and dances, bonfires and traditional games.
mid-June:	**Moncão, Minho** Corpus Christi Festival— procession of oxen, parade of floats, symbolic tournament.
13–28 June:	**Vila Real, Trás-os-Montes** St Anthony and St Peter's Festivals—craft fairs, folk music, fireworks.
12–13, 23–24, 28–29 June:	**Lisbon** 'Popular Saints' Festivals–bonfires of scented herbs, songs and dances.
23–24 June:	**Oporto, Douro** St John's Festival—riotous merry-making, bonfires, singing and dancing, and bashing everyone with leeks. (St John's is also celebrated with major festivals in Évora, Vila do Conde, Braga, Sobrado-Valongo, Figueira de Foz.)
24 June:	**Viseu, Beira Alta** Cavalhadas de Vil de Moinhos— parade of cavalcades, folk song and dance.

28–29 June:	**Póvoa de Varzim, Douro** St Peter's Festival—bonfires, dancing, procession, funfairs.
29 June:	**Sintra, Estremadura** St Peter's Festival—craft fair.
1st weekend in July	**Tómar, Ribatejo** Tabuleiros Festival—(even years): spectacular procession of girls carrying tall baskets of bread and flowers on their heads; folk dancing, fireworks.
July 10–7:	**Coimbra, Beira Litoral** Festival of the Queen Saint—processions, cultural events, funfairs.
1st weekend in July:	**Vila Franca de Xira, Estremadura** Festival of the Red Waistcoats (costume of the *campinos*, horsemen who guard the region's bulls)—bullfights, trials of skill, folk dances.
25 July:	**Anca, Beira Litoral** Festival of St Thomas and St James— farmers' pilgrimage, procession of horse men, parades.
25 July–8 August:	**Sétubal, Estremadura** St James's Fair—funfair, folk dances, exhibitions.
1st Sunday in August:	**Guimarães, Minho** St Walter's Festival—traditional folk processions, funfairs, dancing.
mid-August:	**Portuzelo, Minho** St Martha's Festival—processions and floats, folk costume parade, funfair, blessing of animals.
mid-August:	**Torno, Minho** Festival of Senhora Aparecida—old folk pilgrimage, huge float, fair.
mid-August:	**Póvoa de Varzim, Douro** Festival of the Assumption of Our Lady—blessing of boats, funfair, fireworks, bullfights.

3rd Sunday in August:	**Miranda do Douro, Trás-os-Montes** St Barbara's Festival— famous *pauliteiros* dance.
3rd week in August:	**Viana do Castelo, Minho** Pilgrimage of Our Lady of Sorrows— procession on carpets of flowers, bull running, fireworks, parade of carnival giants and regional costume, folk dances and songs, craft fairs.
1st weekend in September:	**Palmela, Estremadura** Wine Harvest Festival— symbolic treading of grapes, procession and blessing of wine, folk song and dance.
6–8 September:	**Lamego, Beira Alta** Festival of Our Lady of Remedies— pilgrimage, religious procession of floats pulled by oxen, funfairs, fireworks, folk song and dance, exhibitions.
6–8 September:	**Miranda do Douro, Trás-os-Montes** Pilgrimage to Our Lady of Nazo at Povoa—folk pilgrimage, fair.
8–11 September:	**Nazaré, Estremadura** Festival of Our Lady of Nazaré— processions, song and dance, bullfights.
3rd weekend in September:	**Ponte de Lima, Minho** New Fairs—riverside fair, folk music and dancing, procession.
20–26 September:	**Elvas, Alentejo** St Mateus Fair and Festival of Senhor Jesus da Piedade—agricultural fair, processions, riding competitions, folk song and dance, bullfights.
29 September– October:	**Vila Franca de Xira, Estremadura** Autumn 6 Fair—handicrafts, bull running in the streets.
12–13 October:	**Fátima, Ribatejo** Second annual pilgrimage.

16 October:	**Castro Verde, Alentejo** October Fair—handicrafts, traditional entertainment.
19–20 October:	**Tomar, Ribatejo** St Iria's Fair—agricultural fair with handicrafts and seasonal dried fruits.
21 October – 1 November:	**Santarém, Ribatejo** National Gastronomic Festival—food, folk music, handicrafts.
6–11 November:	**Golega, Ribatejo** National Horse Fair—horse parades, bullfights, riding competitions, traditional celebrations.
13 December:	**Freamunde-Pacos de Ferreira, Douro** St Luzia Festival and Capon Fair—old folk pilgrimage, capon sale.

National Holidays

New Year's Day	1 January
Shrove Tuesday	variable
Good Friday	variable
Liberation Day	25 April
May Day	1 May
Corpus Christi	variable
Camões Day	10 June
Assumption of Our Lady	15 August
Republic Day	5 October
All Saints Day	1 November
Independence Day	1 December
Immaculate Conception	8 December
Christmas Day	25 December

Practical Information

Language and Glossary

Portuguese is the seventh most widely spoken language in the world, but that does not make it any easier to pronounce. A knowledge of French, Spanish or Latin can help, though there are still surprises to trip you up—like pronouncing *s* as *sh* before a consonant or at the end of a word (so that 'Cascais', for instance, sounds like 'Kashkaish'). Other little quirks include:

X	is pronounced 'sh'
Q	is pronounced 'k'
C	is soft before 'e' and 'i' but hard before 'a', 'o', and 'u' unless it has a cedilla (e.g. *açucar* is pronounced 'assookar')
Ch	is pronounced 'sh'
Lh	sounds like 'ly'
J	is soft

The tilde over *a* or *o* (or *ão*) creates a more nasal sound (e.g. as in *pão* which sounds like 'pow')

English is spoken in most Algarve resorts and other major tourist centres, though French is more common, especially in the north where farmers in the remotest villages still remember the language after years of work abroad. Even saying 'hello' in Portuguese will bring you great rewards of smiles and friendliness, and if you persevere, phrases will soon come tripping off the tongue.

Essentials

Good morning	*Bom dia*
Good afternoon/evening	*Boa tarde*
Goodnight	*Boa noite*
Goodbye	*Adeus*
Please	*Por favor/se faz favor*
Thank you	*Obrigado* (if spoken by a man)
	Obrigada (if spoken by a woman)
Thank you very much	*Muito obrigado (a)*
yes/no	*sim/não*
Do you speak English?	*Fala Ingles?*
I don't understand	*Não comprendo*
How much?	*Quanto custa?*

Useful Words and Phrases

It's good/OK	*Está bem*
sorry/excuse me	*Desculpe*
where/when/why	*onde/quando/porque*
How are you?	*Como está?*
My name is. . .	*Chamo-me. . .*
What's your name?	*Como se chama?*
today/tomorrow/yesterday	*hoje/amanha/ontem*
here/there	*aqui/ali*
this/that	*este(a)/esse(a)*
big/little	*grande/pequeno*
open/closed	*aberto/fechado*
Where is the toilet?	*Onde ficam os lavabos?*
It's cheap/expensive	*É barato/caro*
I don't want it	*Não o quero*
Please write it for me	*Por favor, escreva*
I'd like. . .	*Queria. . .*
Do you have a double room?	*Tem um quarto duplo?*
with shower/bathroom	*com duche/casa de banho*
May I see the room?	*Posso ver o quarto?*
That's fine	*Está bem*
a few days	*alguns dias*
What do you call this in Portuguese?	*Como se chama isto em Portugues?*
I am English	*Sou Ingles/a*
It's beautiful	*É lindo*

Directions

Where is the railway/bus station?	*Onde é a estação de comboios/de autocarros?*
Where is the bank?	*Onde é o banco?*
How do I get there?	*Como se vai para la?*
Is this the train for. . ?	*É este o comboio para . . ?*
Stop here please	*Pare aqui por favor*
Is there a bus to. . ?	*Há um autocarro para . . .?*
Is there a pension here?	*Há uma pensao aqui?*
Where can I get a taxi?	*Onde posso apanhar um taxi?*
Is there a bus into town?	*Há um autocarro para a cidade?*
Where's the tourist office?	*Onde é o turismo?*

Days of the Week

Sunday	*domingo*
Monday	*segunda-feira*
Tuesday	*terça-feira*
Wednesday	*quarta-feira*
Thursday	*quinta-feira*
Friday	*sexta-feira*
Saturday	*sábado*

Numbers

one	*um*
two	*dois*
three	*três*
four	*quatro*
five	*cinco*
six	*seis*
seven	*sete*
eight	*oito*
nine	*nove*
ten	*dez*
eleven	*onze*
twelve	*doze*
thirteen	*treze*
fourteen	*catorze*
fifteen	*quinze*
sixteen	*dizasseis*
seventeen	*dezassete*
eighteen	*dexoito*
nineteen	*dezanove*
twenty	*vinte*
thirty	*trinta*
forty	*quarenta*
fifty	*cinquenta*
sixty	*sessenta*
seventy	*setenta*
eighty	*oitenta*
ninety	*noventa*
one hundred	*cem*
five hundred	*quinhentos*
one thousand	*mil*

Places

tourist office	*turismo*
bank	*banco*
post office	*correios*
church	*igreja*
museum	*museu*
beach	*praia*
police station	*o Posto da Polícia*
hospital	*hospital*
town hall	*câmara municipal*
square	*largo/praça/campo*
market	*mercado*
chemist	*farmaceûtico*

Shopping

Do you sell. . . ?	*Vendem. . . ?*
It's very expensive	*É muito caro*
Do you have any postcards?	*Tem postais?*
I'm just looking	*Estou só a ver*
I'd like. . .	*Queria. . .*
How much is this?	*Quanto é isto?*
Do you have anything cheaper?	*Não tem nada mais barato?*
I'll take it	*Fico com ele*
Can I pay by traveller's cheque?	*Posso pagar com um cheque de viagem?*
Do you have films for this camera?	*Tem filmes para esta máquina?*
A stamp for this postcard, please	*Um selo para este postal, por favor*

Restaurant and Menu

menu	*ementa*
the bill	*a conta*
the wine list	*a lista dos vinhos*
red wine/white wine	*vinho tinto/vinho branco*
house wine	*vinho da casa*
Is service included?	*O serviço está incluido?*
breakfast/lunch/dinner	*pequeno almoço/almoço/jantar*
dish of the day	*prato do dia*

Basics

Tea/coffee	*Chá/café*
small black coffee	*bica*
large white coffee	*galão*
beer	*cerveja*
mineral water	*água mineral*
bread	*pão*
cheese	*queijo*
salt/pepper	*sal/pimenta*

Fish and Shellfish

salted cod	*bacalhau*
sole	*linguado*
hake	*pescada*
mackerel	*carapaus*
sardines	*sardinhas*
trout	*truta*
squid	*lula*
tuna	*atum*
clams	*ameijoas*
seafood paella	*arroz de marisco*
mussels	*mexilhões*
shrimps	*camarões*
prawns	*gambas*
Algarve dish of pressure-cooked clams with bacon, sausages, peppers	*Cataplana*

Poultry and Meat

chicken	*frango*
turkey	*peru*
veal	*vitela*
sausage	*salsicha*
suckling pig	*leitão*
pork	*porco*
steak	*bife*
kid	*cabrito*
lamb	*anho*
liver	*fígado*

Basic Vocabulary

**P**ick up any guidebook to Portugal and there will be a simplistic essay—either by some British pundit or by some Portuguese journalist looking to make a few escudos—on the subject of our national character. Invariably you will find the same set of words.

Siso *and* loucura: *The former is something like prudence, and the latter is excess, a flair for the quixotic (even though Quixote was Spanish), both of which are presumably at war in the Portuguese soul.*

Saudade: *This word, also difficult to translate into any other language, suggests our melancholy yearning for past glories. The Greeks, too, have some of this, but they tend to be more cheerful than we. If one were to suppose a Greek at work in his American diner or pizza parlor or resting from his labors on a construction job in Australia but in either case muttering lines from Aeschylus and Sophocles and blaming himself for having fallen from such heights to this present and altogether regrettable condition, then he'd qualify. And there would be a word in Greek that means* saudade. *(But if there is, I'm not familiar with it.)*

Sebastianismo: *This is the winner, the killer, the one that has most to do with Salazar. This is the secret belief that somehow or other the old days will return, that Sebastian, who was not actually seen to have been killed at Alcácer–Kebir in 1578, is hiding out somewhere and may at any moment turn a corner and come riding down some hill into his old palace courtyard in Lisbon.*

The worst of it is that these writers of tourist book essays are correct. Those are the words, and that is the character of our people.

I suppose that another word might be added:

Salazarismo: *This means either the belief out there in the country that Salazar may at any moment return to his office and offices. Or, alternatively, Salazar's own belief that he is still running the country.*

David Slavitt, Salazar Blinks

Terms of Cooking

roasted	*assado*
boiled	*cozido*
fried	*frito*
grilled	*grelhado*
baked	*no forno*

Vegetables and Fruit

rice	*arroz*
potatoes	*batatas*
salad	*salada*
beans	*feijão*
carrots	*cenouras*
onions	*cebolas*
tomatoes	*tomates*
peas	*ervilhas*
vegetarian dishes	*pratos vegetarianos*
orange	*laranja*
lemon	*limão*
apple	*maçã*
strawberries	*morangos*
grapes	*uvas*
figs	*figos*

Glossary

albufeira	reservoir
alameda	promenade
azulejo	glazed tiles
andar	storey
bairro	quarter of a town
barragem	dam
baixa	shopping centre of a town
Camara Municipal	town hall
capela	chapel
castelo	castle, citadel
citânia	prehistoric settlement
cruz	cross
ermida	remote chapel
grutas	caves

igreja matriz	parish (mother) church
miradouro	viewpoint
mosteiro	monastery
mudéjar	Moorish-style architecture or decoration
paco/pálacio	palace or mansion
pelourinho	stone pillory
quinta	country villa
Sé	cathedral
solar	manor house
torre de menagem	keep of a castle
tumulo	tomb

Useful Addresses

Tourist Offices

There are **Turismo** offices in almost every town in Portugal, offering help with maps, information and local hotel bookings. They are officially open Monday to Saturday from 9 am to 6 pm, although this varies from place to place; in practice 10 am–noon, 2 pm–5 pm Monday to Friday are more reliable opening times.

Lisbon
Praça dos Restauradores, tel. 01-3463643/3463658/363624

Oporto
Praça do General Humberto Delgado, tel. 02-312740
Praça Dom João I, tel. 02-37154/313957

Algarve

Albufeira Rua 5 de Outoubro, tel. 089-52144
Faro 8 Rua da Misericórdia, tel. 089-25404
Lagos Largo Marquês de Pombal, tel. 082-57728
Loulé Castle, tel. 089-63900
Portimão Largo do 1 de Dezembro, tel. 082-23695
Silves Rua 25 de Abril, tel. 082-42255
Tavira Praça da República, tel. 081-22511
Vila Real de Santo Antonio Praça Marquês de Pombal, tel. 081-44495/43772

Alentejo

Beja 25 Rua do Capitao J F de Sousa, tel. 084-23693
Castelo de Vide 81 Rua de Bartolomeu Alvares da Santa, tel. 045-91361
Elvas Praça da República, tel. 068-62236
Estremoz 26 Largo da República
Évora Praça do Giraldo, tel. 066-22671
Marvão Rua Dr Matos Magalhaes, tel. 045-93226
Portalegre 40 Rua 19 de Junho, tel. 045-21815
Serpa 2 Largo Dom Jorge de Melo, tel. 084-52335

Estremadura and Ribatejo

Alcobaça Praça 25 de Abril, tel. 062-42377
Caldas da Rainha Praça da República, tel. 062-22400
Estoril Arcadas do Parque, tel. 01-2680113
Obidos Rua Direita, tel. 062-95234
Santarém 63 Rua de Capelo Ivens, tel. 043-23140
Sesimbra Avenida dos Naufragos, tel. 01-2233304
Setubal Largo do Corpo Santo, tel. 065-24284
Sintra 3 Praça da República, tel. 01-2931157
Tomar Avenida Dr Candido Madureira, tel. 043-33095

The Beiras

Aveiro Praça da República, tel. 034-22571
Castelo Branco Alameda da Liberdade, tel. 072-21002
Coimbra Largo da Portagem, tel. 039-23799
Covhilha Town Hall, tel. 075-22170
Figueira da Foz Rua 25 de Abril, tel. 033-22610
Guarda Praça de Luís de Camões, tel. 071-22251
Leiria Jardim Luís Camões, tel. 044-22748
Viseu Avenida Calouste Gulbenkian, tel. 032-22294

The Douro

Amarante Rua Cândido dos Reis, tel. 055-42980
Lamego Avenida Visconde Guedes Teixeira, tel. 054-62005
Povoa de Varzim 166 Avenida Mouzinho de Albuquerque, tel. 052-64609
Vila do Conde Rua 25 de Abril, tel. 052-63427

The Minho

Barcelos   Rua Duques de Bragança, tel. 053-82882
Braga   Avenida Liberdade, tel. 053-22550
Guimarães   83 Avenida Resistencia aõ Fascismo, tel. 053-42450
Monção   Largo de Loreto, tel. 051-52647
Viana do Castelo   Avenida Cândido dos Reis, tel. 058-22620

Trás-os-Montes

Bragança   Largo do Principal, tel. 073-22271/23078
Chaves   213 Rua de Santo Antonio, tel. 076-21029
Vila Real   70 Avenida 1 de Maio, tel. 059-22819

Overseas Portuguese National Tourist Offices

Amsterdam   Stadhouderskade 57, tel. 750301
Barcelona   7 Ronda de San Pedro, tel. 750301
Brussels   129-A Avenida Louise Laan, tel. 17-435900
Dublin   c/o Portuguese Embassy, Knocksinna House, Knocksinna, Fox Rock, Dublin 18, tel. 893569
Frankfurt   66 Kaiserstrasse, tel. 234094
Geneva   50 Quai Gustave Ador, tel. 7861460
London   1-5 New Bond Street, London, tel. 071-493 3873
Madrid   27 Gran Via, tel. 5229354
Milan   2 Via Gonzaga, tel. 866678
Montreal   500 Sherbrooke W Suite 930, tel. 8434623
New York   590 Fifth Avenue, tel. 354-4403
Paris   7 Rue Scribe, tel. 47425557
Stockholm   2 Linnegatan, S.11447, tel. 6602654
Tokyo   101 Regency Shinsaka, 8-5-8 Akasaka, Minato-ku, tel. 5474-4400
Toronto   4120 Yonge Street, Suite 414 Willowdale, tel. 250-7575

Embassies in Lisbon

Australia   244 Avenida da Liberdade, tel. 523350
Austria   70 Rua das Amoreiras, tel. 654161
Belgium   14 Praça Marques de Pombal, tel. 549263
Canada   2 Rua Rosa Araujo, tel. 563821
Denmark   14 Rua Castilho, tel. 545099

France 5 Rua dos SantosucVelho, tel. 608121
Great Britain 35 Rua Sao Domingos à Lapa, tel. 661191/661122
Ireland 1 Rua da Imprensa, tel. 661569
Italy 6 Largo Conde Pombeiro, tel. 546144
Japan 14 Avenida Fontes Pereira de Melo, tel. 562177
Spain 1 Rua do Salitre, tel. 372381
United States Avenida das Forças Armadas, tel. 726660

Railway stations

Lisbon - Santa Apolónia, tel. 01-864143/876025
Rossio, tel. 01-3465022
Terreiro do Paço Fluvial, tel. 01-367631

Oporto - Campanha, tel. 02-565645
São Bento, tel. 02-319517/311616
Trinidade, tel. 02-25224

Airports

Lisbon Portela, tel. 01-802060/8485974
Oporto Pedras Rubras, tel. 02-9482141

Airlines

TAP–Air Portugal Rua D. Francisco Gomes, Faro, tel. 089-22141; 3 Praça Marquês de Pombal, Lisbon, tel. 01-544080; Praça Mouzinho de Albuquerque, Oporto, tel. 02-696041

British Airways 36 Avenida da Liberdade, Lisbon, tel. 01-3460931; 778 Praceta Eng. Amaro da Costa, Oporto, tel. 02-9481989

Air France 244 Avenida da Liberdade, Lisbon, tel. 01-562171; 663 Rua de Sta. Catarina, Oporto, tel. 02-313363

Lufthansa 192A Avenida da Liberdade, Lisbon, tel. 01-573852; 1681 Avenida da Boavista, Oporto, tel. 02-667006

TWA 258A Avenida da Liberdade, Lisbon, tel. 01-527141; 585 Julio Dinis, Oporto, tel. 02-6000863/691335

Car Hire

British visitors who plan to hire a car in Portugal may find prices are lower at home. In the UK, travel agencies such as F D Travel (tel. 0277-372339), tour companies with fly-drive deals and major car hire firms can arrange prior bookings.

Within Portugal, all the major firms (Avis, Hertz, Kenning, Europcar, etc.) are represented at the airports in Faro, Lisbon and Oporto as well as at major hotels and the following offices:

Faro
Europcar, tel. 089-818777

 (Two cheaper local firms are Jante Internacional, Avenida 5 de Outubro, Faro, tel. 089-812265; and RMS, 32 Rua C. Bivar, Faro, tel. 081-81334.)

Lisbon
Avis, 47 Praça dos Restauradores, tel. 01-361171
Kenning, 4 Rua Luciano Cordeiro, tel. 01-549182
Europcar, 24 Avenida Antonio Augusto de Aguiar, tel. 01-524558
Hertz, 10 Avenida 5 de Outubro, tel. 01-579027

Oporto
Avis, 125 Guedes de Azevedo, tel. 02-315947
Hertz, 899 Rua de Santa Catarina, tel. 02-9481400

Bragança
Ceuta Rent-a-Car, Novo Mundo Viagens e Turismo, tel. 073-22636

The Portuguese Automobile Club
24 Rua Rosa Araujo, Lisbon, tel. 01-736121;
2-6 Rua Goncalo Cristovao, Oporto, tel. 02-316732.

Hospitals

Lisbon British Hospital, 49 Rua Saraiva de Carvalho, tel. 01-602020/603785
for English-speaking service.

Oporto Santo António Hospital, tel. 02-27354
Emergency tel. 115

Accommodation

While you can still find some of Europe's best-value-for-money accommodation in Portugal, prices are quickly catching up. In high season (June/July to September), expect prices to almost double.

If money is no problem, and you are after something uniquely Portuguese, you can do no better than head for the famous government-owned *pousadas* (similar to the Spanish *paradors*), or the lesser-known *Turismo de Habitação* private manor houses.

There are 30 **pousadas** scattered throughout the country, nearly half of them in converted castles, monasteries or palaces (the ones at Estremoz, Óbidos and Évora are outstanding examples), and all of them in places of historic interest or scenic beauty. They are priced (including breakfast) according to three categories, B, C, and CH. For high season (1 July to 30 September) in 1990, rates for double rooms were as follows: Es. 9,000 (B); Es.12,900 (C); Es.17,500 (CH). Advance bookings (months ahead for high season) are essential for the most popular *pousadas*. Contact: ENATUR, Empresa Nacional de Turismo, E P, 10 Av. Santa Joana à Princesa, 1700 Lisboa (tel. 881221, or 889078; telex 13609 ENATUR P).

The **Turismo de Habitação** scheme is an upper-class kind of bed-and-breakfast system whereby luxurious accommodation is offered in private manor houses and stately farms (some with self-catering facilities, like the French *gîtes*). It operates under a confusing variety of names *(Turismo no Espaço Rural, A Tradição de Portugal, Associação das Casas do Turismo de Habitação),* but the idea is the same, and prices are similar, although the Associação do Turismo de Habitação operates only in the north, particularly the Minho region. For details and reservations, contact TURIHAB (Associação do Turismo de Habitação), Praça da República, 4990 Ponte de Lima (tel. 058-942729; telex 32618 PTPL P) and/or A Tradição de Portugal, Promocoes e Ideias Turisticas, S A, Alto da Pampilheira, Torre D-2, 8 A 2750 Cascais (tel. 2867958; telex 43304 PITSA P).

Bookings can also be made on the spot through local Turismo offices (the official requirement to stay a minimum of three nights and pay in advance is not enforced in this case). Make sure you get a map as these private houses are not as well sign-posted as *pousadas*. Prices vary according to the luxury of the tapestries, leather chairs, four-poster beds, roaring log fires, baronial credentials, etc. but expect a double in high season to range between Es.9,000 and Es.15,000.

Ordinary hotels seem very ordinary after this. But there is plenty of choice: *estalagems* and *albergarias* are privately-run inns, usually of a high standard, with prices in the moderate to expensive bracket (Es.8,000–Es.15,000 for double in high season). **Hotels** are rated from one to five stars and usually have more facilities and higher prices than *residencials*, which are rated from one to four stars.

The stars and ratings are best ignored: many *residencials* and even the cheaper *pensãos* (one to four stars) can be a lot better than a one- or two-star hotel. A high-season double in a clean and friendly *pensão*, the best budget choice, rarely costs more than Es.4,000. In seaside resorts and tourist locations, there are often even cheaper private rooms (*quartos* or *dormidas*) available— wait to be accosted at bus stations or ask for a list at the Turismo office.

The following recommendations are rated according to prices for a double in high season 1990:
Expensive: Es. 11,000–15,000 and over (Very Expensive)
Moderate: Es. 6,000–11,000
Cheap: Es. 2,000–6,000

Not only are prices different in high season; within hotels there is a range of prices depending on whether the room has a private bath or a good view—check out the options. Budget travellers will usually find the lowest category room perfectly adequate.

The Algarve

Albufeira

Hotel Rocamar Rua Jacinto D'Ayet (tel. 089-53599). Has rather tasteless decor but its location, right on the beach, is superb. Expensive.
Pensão Vila Recife Rua Miguel Bombarda (tel. 089-52047). Looks like a charming little private house but inside business is brisk, with nearly 200 rooms. Moderate.

Caldas de Monchique

Pensão Central Central square (tel. 082-92203). Tucked in a moist green eucalyptus dingle at the heart of a half-forgotten Victorian spa. Its floors are bare, its bathtubs huge, its bowls of flowers fragrant and wilted. An Afghan hound and Siamese cat wander around the excellent (and surprisingly smart) restaurant. Cheap.

Faro

Hotel Eva Avenida da República (tel. 089-803354). Has the best harbour spot in town and a throbbing disco. Expensive.
Hotel Faro Praça Dr Francisco Gomes (tel. 089-22076). A dull sort of place but some rooms do overlook the harbour. Moderate.
Pensão Madelena 109 Rua Conselheiro Bivar (tel. 089-20806). Popular and well run, with new pine furnishings, although the downstairs rooms can be dark and noisy. Cheap.

Lagos

Hotel de Lagos Rua Nova da Aldeia (tel. 082-62011). Very discreet and tasteful, with an abundance of greenery, fountains, and elegant white and chrome decor. Very expensive.
Albergaria Marina-Rio Avenida dos Descobrimentos (tel. 082-769749). Unattractively located beside the bus station, but new, fresh, and away from the congestion of town. Moderate.
Hotel Riomar Rua Cândido dos Reis (tel. 082-63091). Next to a funky (and defunct) 1920s cinema in the town centre; has rather dowdy decor but is friendly and popular with the British. Moderate.
Pensão Caravela Avenida 25 de Abril (tel. 082-62949). Not recommended by Turismo, but I found nothing wrong, except the rooms are box-size. Cheap.

Olhão

Pensão Bicuar 5 Rua Vasco da Gama (tel. 089-74816). Has the best views in town of the surrounding Moorish white houses. Fussily furnished with plastic flowers and frilly mats; only drawback for insomniacs is a nearby bell-tower, chiming twice every hour.

Sagres

Fortaleza de Beliche (tel. 082-64124). An exclusive outpost (with only eight rooms) in a chic, ancient fort near the headland where Prince Henry the Navigator had his school of navigation. Run by the *pousada* organization; a better deal than the twentieth-century *pousada* in town. Expensive.
Youth Hostel (open summer only, tel. 082-64129). Inside the huge headland Fortaleza, said to be on the very site of Henry's school. Spartan and windswept but great for ghosts and atmosphere. Cheap.

Tavira

Pensão Princesa do Gilão Rua Bord'Agua de Aguiar (tel. 081-23171). Easily recognized on its excellent riverside location by its solar heating panels. Clean, popular and cheap.

The Alentejo

Beja

Residencial Cristina 71 Rua de Mértola (tel. 084-23035). Neat and clean. Moderate.
Pensão Rocha 12 Rua Dom Nuno Alvares Pereira (tel. 084-24271). A rambling old mansion with pots of character, fresh flowers and cold water. Cheap.

Castelo de Vide

Albergaria Jardim 6 Rua Sequeira Sameiro (tel. 045-91217). Far preferable to the package-tour Sol e Serra Hotel nearby. Intimate and pretty. Cheap.
Residencial Casa do Parque Avenida da Aramanha (tel. 045-91250). Small and friendly with corridors of potted plants and paintings. Favoured guests are given a cockerel memento when they leave. Cheap.

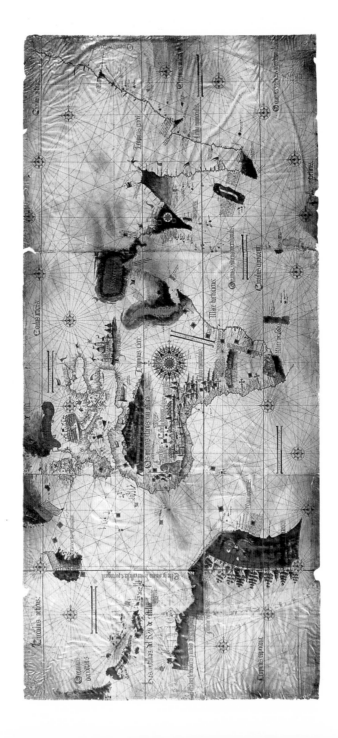

Estremoz

Pousada da Rainha Santa Isabel (tel. 068-22618). The restored thirteenth-century fortress home of King Dinis, and one of the most exquisite *pousadas* in the country, spacious and richly furnished. Very expensive.
Residencial Café Alentejano 15 Rossio (tel. 068-22834). A hive of activity on Saturday market days and a bargain to boot. The marble stairway is deceptive: rooms are clean but basic. Cheap.

Évora

Pousada dos Lóios Largo Conde de Vila Flor (tel. 066-24051). An exclusive haven of luxury, converted from a fifteenth-century monastery around a delightful cloister. Pity the staff are so stuffy. Very expensive.
Residencial O Eborense 1 Largo da Misericordia (tel. 066-22031). One of the best bargains in Portugal. The former sixteenth-century mansion of Count Monfalim sports a marble stairway, garden and pretty loggia. Not surprisingly, rooms are hard to get. Cheap.
Pensão Policarpo 16 Rua da Freira de Baixo (tel. 066-22424). Another 16th-century mansion, its downstairs rooms are a bit pokey, but upstairs can get positively grand. Breakfast of bread and honey is served in a rustic, cosy salon with glazed pottery, *azulejos* on the walls and a singing waitress. Cheap.

Marvão

Pousada de Santa Maria 7 Rua 24 de Janeiro (tel. 045-93201). Reflects all the charm of Marvão, with local decor and cosy bedrooms. Expensive.

Estremadura and the Ribatejo

Alcobaça

Pensão Mosteiro 5 Rua Estêvão Martins (tel. 062-42183). Cheap and cheerful, although its restaurant is aiming for greater things, with an overpriced menu and waitress in red stilettoes and mini-skirt. Cheap.

Lisbon

The Ritz Intercontinental 88 Rua Rodrigo da Fonsêça (tel. 01-692020; telex 12589 RITZ P). Very plush indeed, with 1950s decor titillated by modern sculptures and tapestries. Very expensive.
Hotel Eduardo VII 5 Avenida Fontes Pereira de Melo (tel. 01-530141;

telex. 18340 EDUTEL P). An old favourite (though located on a noisy main road), with charming staff in the traditional mould. Expensive.

Hotel Suisso-Atlantico 3 Rua Glória (tel. 01-3461713). Tatty in parts, but its quiet, central location is hard to beat. Moderate.

Hotel Jorge V 3 Rua Mousinho da Silveira (tel. 01-562525). Still quaint and cosy despite its faded decor. Moderate.

Pensão Londres 53 Rua Dom Pedro V (tel. 01-3462203). One of the best pensions in town, in a good location at the top of the Gloria Elevador. Rooms are light and high-ceilinged with tremendous views. Cheap.

Within walking distance of the Rossio are dozens of **cheap pensions**, often in upper floors of old tenement blocks. Some areas (like the Praça da Alegria) are in a sleazier business than tourism but can provide harmless rock-bottom-price rooms. The **Turismo** in Praça dos Restauradores can make recommendations and bookings if you are after something slightly more respectable.

Óbidos

Pousada do Castelo (tel. 062-95105, telex. 15540). Small, nestled at the far end of the old walled citadel; complements its medieval surroundings with suits of armour and glowing wood furnishings. Very expensive.

Casa de Hóspedes Madeira Rua Direita (tel. 062-95212). One of the few cheaper options within the walls. Aspidistras on the stone steps and old-fashioned washbasins in the cosy rooms give it oodles of character. Cheap.

Sintra

Hotel Palácio de Seteais 8 Avenida Barbosa Bocage (tel. 01-9233200; fax 01-9234277). A former eighteenth century manor house in palatial style, its lounge sporting walls (and piano) painted with rural scenes. The right wing is under restoration. Very expensive.

Hotel Tivoli Sintra Praça da República (tel. 01-9233505). An agreeable, more central alternative. Expensive.

Pensão Casa Adelaide 11 Avenida Guilherme Gomes Fernandes (tel. 01-9230873). Probably the best of the cheapies.

Byron *aficionados* may want to check whether the poet's former hostel, the **Estalagem Cavaleiros,** has yet been restored; neglected for years and almost in ruins, it was due to be revived in 1991.

Tomar

Hotel dos Templários 1 Largo Cândido dos Reis (tel. 049-32121). Has fine views of the famous Convento, but for a quieter location check to see if the

Estalagem de Santa Iria (Parque do Mouchao) has opened after renovation. Both are moderate.
Pensão Nuno Álvares 3 Avenida Nuno Alvares. On a busy main road but its comfortable rooms are the best bargain in town. Cheap.

The Beiras

Aveiro
Hotel Imperial Rua Dr Nascimento Leitão (tel. 034-22141; fax 034-24148). Favoured by tour groups for its excellent location above the Central Canal, and neat, jazzy decor. Moderate.
Residencial Palmeira 7–11 Rua da Palmeira (tel. 034-22521). Centrally located in a quiet back street, friendly, and family-run, with spick-and-span modern rooms. Cheap.

Coimbra

Hotel Astoria 21 Avenida Emídio Navarro (tel. 039-22055). A must for 1930s nostalgics, with its mirrored walls, pearl-drop chandeliers, old wireless sets and tinted photos. Only the staff exhibit modern trends in surliness. Moderate.
Residencial Larbelo 33 Largo da Portagem (tel. 039-29092). Pleasant and cheap.
Residencial Hospédaria Simões 69 Rua Fernandes Tomás (tel. 039-34638). Tucked away in the old town and excellent value. Get a street-facing room and you may be serenaded at night by local *fado* singers. Cheap.

Covilha

Residencial Santa Eufemia Sítio da Palmatoria (tel. 075-26081). Not very central but pleasantly furnished, with nice views. Cheap.

Figueira da Foz

Hotel Universal 50 Rua Miguel Bombarda (tel. 033-26228). A fine hotel, much liked by Europeans. Moderate.
Pensão Residencial Europa 40 Rua Cândido dos Reis. Even closer to the casino, and full of diehard gamblers. Cheap.

Leiria

Hotel Dom João III Avenida Herois de Angola (tel. 044-33902). The best in town, though not very central. Moderate.
Hotel Liz 10 Largo Alexandre Herculano (tel. 044-31017). Overlooks the main square, is adequate but nothing special. Moderate.

Residencial Casa de Santo António 10A Rua Machado dos Santos (tel. 044-22150). Up three flights of stairs with pretty murals. Tiny rooms lead off a narrow, well-adorned corridor. Adequate and cheap.

Luso

The Palace Hotel Mata do Buçaco (tel. 031-93101). *The* place to stay in Buçaco's mystical forest. A neo-Manueline fantasy of wriggling arches, stairways of *azulejos* and pirouettes of carved stone everywhere. Fantastic and very expensive.

Viseu

Pensão Rossio Parque 55 Rua Soar de Cima (tel. 032-25785). Delightful, from its immaculately patched and polished red lino on the stairs to the statuettes in the corridors and old-fashioned screens to hide the washbasins in the bedrooms. Cheap.

The Douro

Amarante

Hotel Silva 53 Rua Cândido dos Reis (tel. 055-423110). Superb riverside location with a wisteria-covered terrace which more than compensates for the rather small rooms. Cheap.

Lamego

Albergaria do Cerrado Lugar do Cerrado (tel. 054-63154). Sunny-coloured, bright and cheerful, with double-glazing to keep out traffic noise. Moderate.
Pensão Silva 26 Rua Tras de Sé (tel. 054-62929). Right by the cathedral, has a brusque manageress, but rooms have nice old-fashioned touches (Venetian blinds, screens, bare floorboards). Cheap.

Oporto

Hotel Infante de Sagres 62 Praça D. Filipa de Lancastre (tel. 02-2008101; fax 02-314937). The unrivalled best, with deluxe furnishings and surprisingly un-snooty staff. Very expensive.
Hotel Castor 17 Rua das Doze Casas (tel. 02-570014). Not exactly central, but a popular choice, pleasantly furnished. Expensive.
Hotel São Joãoz 120 Rua do Bonjardim (tel. 02-21662). Right in the heart of town, efficient and comfortable. Moderate.
Residencial São Marino 59 Praça Carlos Alberto (tel. 02-325499). Crisp and neat, a favourite with Portuguese businessmen. Cheap.
Residencial Pão-de-Açar 262 Rua do Almada (tel. 02-22425). Boasts 'traquility absolute' (sic) despite its busy location. Cheap.
Pensão Novo Mundo 92 Rua Conde de Vizela (tel. 02-25403). Good value: friendly, central and with some surprisingly quiet rooms (try 6 or 7). Cheap.
Pensão de Norte 579 Rua Fernando Tomás (tel. 02-23503). Looks the pits (some would say it is) but its shabby old rooms (complete with frilly pink bedcovers) are big and fun. Dirt cheap.
Pensão Astória 56 Rua Arnaldo Gama (tel. 02-28175). Would be wonderful if you could get a room: a charming old house just outside the city walls, with tranquility and river views. Try booking ahead. Cheap.

The Minho

Barcelos

Pensão Bagoeira 57 Avenida Dr Sidónio Pais (tel. 053-82236). Overpriced and extremely frilly but you forgive everything on account of its wonderful hubbub on market days. Cheap.

Braga

Residencial Grande Avenida 738 Avenida da Liberdade (tel. 053-22955). A variety of good value rooms. Cheap.
Hotel Francfort Avenida Central (tel. 053-22648). Pricier than it deserves—you pay for its seedy charm, friendly old manageress and view over the central square. Cheap.
Hotel do Elevador Bom Jesus (tel. 053-25011). A better bet for comfort than anything in Braga, plus you get the views. Moderate.

Caldas do Gerês

Hotel do Parque Avenida Manuel Francisco da Costa (tel. 053-39112). Ageing gracefully, like others in town, and a dream bargain out of season. Moderate.
Pensão da Ponte (tel. 053-39121). Has rambling corridors of neat little rooms and a lobby of spa patients knitting as they watch TV; its newly built **Residencial Principe** nearby offers bigger, modern rooms, no geriatric knitters and river sounds at night. Both cheap.

Guimaraes

Pousada de N.S. da Oliveira (tel. 053-412157). In the style of a baronial mansion, at the historic heart of town. Expensive.
Pousada de Santa Marinha (tel. 053-418453). The one you always see on posters—an incredibly grand converted twelfth-century monastery in the Penha National Park a few kilometres from Guimarães. Very expensive.
Casa de Retiros 163 Rua Francisco Agra (tel. 053-511515). A church hostel; neat, simple and efficiently run by the Missionários Redentoristas. Laudably cheap.

Monção

Pensão Central Praça Deu-la-Deu (tel. 051-52222). Has laundry hanging in the stairwell and beds whose springs have seen better days but all worth bearing for the balcony rooms overlooking the square. Cheap.

Ponte de Barça

Pensão Gomes 13 Rua Conselheiro Rocha Peixoto (tel. 058-42288). A gem: its four little attic rooms (two overlooking the river) have olde worlde wash-stands and shiny wooden floors. Cheap.

Ponte de Lima

Pensão São João 6 Rua do Rosario (tel. 058-941288). Centres around its warm, busy kitchen. Good rooms, good food, good price. Cheap.

Viana do Castelo

Hotel de Santa Luzia (tel. 058-828889; telex 32420). On the quiet hilltop above Viana, sports an elegant art deco look. Expensive.
Residencial Viana Mar 215 Avenida Combatentes da Grande Guerra (tel. 058-828962). Central, clean and comfortable with a striking fondness for plastic flowers. Cheap.

Entrada da Barra, *Carlos Botelho, 1964 (above)*
Auto-retrato num grupo, *Almada Negreiros, 1925 (below)*

Trás-os-Montes

Bragança

Pousada de São Bartolomeu Estrada de Turismo (tel. 073-22493). Bags the best view of Bragança's old citadel. Homely, like a country inn, with open fires and looms in the lobby. Moderate.
Pensão Rucha 42 Rua Almirante Reis (tel. 073-22672). Full of roses and friendliness; a troika of women run the place from their huge old kitchen (the grandmother cossets solo travellers with vast breakfasts). Cheap.

Chaves

Hotel Aquae Flaviae Praça do Brasil (tel. 076-26711). New and flashy, catering for wealthy spa visitors. Expensive.
Hotel Trajano Travessa Cândido dos Reis (tel. 076-22425). Nothing special but rooms are pleasantly furnished and staff pleasant. Cheap.
Hotel de Chaves Rua 25 de Abril (tel. 076-21118). An old dame rambling and run-down with a raggedness still beguiling. Cheap.

Freixo de Espada-à-Cinta

Pensão Tavares 35 Rua de Carrascal. The newest pension in town, a private house tucked away in a tiny back-street. Cakes and port come with supper; braying of donkeys with nightfall. Cheap.

Miranda do Douro

Pousada de Santa Catarina (tel. 073-42255; telex 22388). Has a prime view of the dramatic Douro Gorge and a cosy ambience. Moderate.
Pensão Santa Cruz 61 Rua Abade de Baçal (tel. 073-42474). The only guest-house within the old citadel; full of family clutter (including a talking parrot in the breakfast room) but with neat, modern rooms. Cheap.

Montalegre

Residencial Fidalgo Rua do Corujeira (tel. 076-52462). Above town, adorned with lots of incongruous fancy frills. Cheap.

Recommended Restaurants

Hearty helpings and reasonable prices characterize Portuguese restaurants. You can eat well for very little—even if you order a *meia dose* (half portion), an accepted practice. Travellers with good appetites and/or no Portuguese will find the all-inclusive three-course tourist menus useful, but it is always worth checking out the *prata do dia* (dish of the day). Budget diners should look out for the excellent Casa de Pasto restaurants which serve good meals (invariably with TV accompaniment) for rarely more than Es.1,200 per person (including a standard *vinho da casa* wine). The following restaurants are rated according to the average price of a main dish:

Expensive: over Es.1,000
Moderate: Es. 650–1,000
Cheap: under Es.650

Aveiro

O Mercantel Rua de Antonio dos Santos. Close to the fish market; great for fish-lovers and for holding celebrations (the restaurant is accustomed to hosting big parties).
Telheiro 20 Largo da Praça do Peixe (tel. 034-29473). Cosy, with wood benches under hanging hams and bay leaves. The eel stew (an Aveiro speciality) slips down a treat. Moderate.

Beja

Restaurante Tomás 7-11 Rua Alexandre Herculano (tel. 084-24613). Serves a good selection of Alentejan specialities. Moderate.
Casa Primavera 19 Largo do Correio. An unassuming little place with knock-out food; try the local favourite, roast kid *(cabrito)* and chips.

Braga

Inácio 4 Campo das Hortas (tel. 053-22335). Tops the list for quality of food, if not for atmosphere. Moderate.
Restaurant A Ceia Rua do Raio. Makes a pleasant change from tourist traps. A local favourite for its fast and friendly service. Cheap.

Bragança

Lá em Casa Rua Marquês de Pombal (tel. 073-22111). Bow-tied waiters, shiny pine furnishings and an imaginative menu, but the house wine is overpriced. Moderate.

Castelo de Vide

Albergaria Jardim 6 Rua Sequeira Sameiro (tel. 045-91217). Pleasant in all respects (even the TV is out of sight). Moderate.

Os Amigos Rua de Bartolomeu Álvares da Santa, in the main pillory square. A real locals' den, with just one table at the back of the bar and a delicious sizzling speciality the tattooed chef simply calls 'beefsteak pork'. Cheap.

Caldas de Monchique

Restaurante Central Pensão Central (see Accommodation, page 176). Has great character and surprisingly high standards. Try fillet of pork with almonds and apple sauce. Moderate.

Chaves

Restaurant Campismo Largo de São Roque (tel. 076-22912). Patronized by campers from across the road; food here is excellent value-for-money. Go early to get a table. Cheap.

Coimbra

Zé Manuel 12 Beco do Forno (tel. 039-23790). Discriminates against foreigners (Portuguese-speakers only upstairs) but if you can squeeze in downstairs, the food and arty atmosphere is worth the humiliation. Cheap.
Restaurant Funchal 18 Rua das Azeileiras (tel. 039-24137). Quiet, polite and rather dull. Moderate.
Restaurant João Brasileiro 109 Praça do Comércio (tel. 039-22205). Draws a lively crowd of locals with its fast service and bargain food. Cheap.

Ericeira

Mar a Vista Largo das Ribas. Serves really fresh fish—choose your own (live) victim and wait for it to be cooked. Moderate.

Estremoz

Pousada da Rainha Santa Isabel The *pousada's* regal restaurant offers a superb menu suitable for a splurge (fillets of sole with champagne, perhaps?) Expensive.
Arlequim Restaurant 15 Rua Dr Gomes de Resende. A bright and popular little place, run by an ex-pianist and his French wife (she is the cook). Cheap.

Évora

A Cozinha de Santo Humberto 39 Rua da Moeda (tel. 066-24251). Generous helpings of ambience and good food. Expensive.

Almedina 5 Travessa de Santa Marta (tel. 066-20747). Cosy and intimate, with batik tablecloths and crickets serenading you from the little garden out back. The *miga alentejana* is a filling rural speciality. Moderate.

Faro

Casa de Pasto 55 Rua de Sao Pedro. An unpretentious locals' favourite (no English spoken), with simple fare. Cheap.

Cidade Velha 19 Rua Domingos Gueiro (tel. 089-27145). The poshest place in town, twee and romantic, with fancy dishes. Expensive.

Guimarães

Restaurante Bom Retiro Rua Dr Avelino Germano, off Rua da Rainha. Keeps a low profile: a tiny locals' den, with a barrel of red wine in the corner (served into white mugs), raucous repartee, knick-knacks on the walls, and good, honest food. Cheap.

Lagos

O Castelo Rua 25 de Abril. A friendly place, Moderate.

Lamego

O Combinado 89 Rua da Olario (tel. 054-62902). Tries a little too hard to impress, considering its squashed setting, but the local speciality, *truta do rio recheada com presunto* (trout stuffed with smoked ham) is done well. Cheap.

Restaurant & Bar Central de Camionagem Attached to the bus station. This bright Californian-decor restaurant not only looks nice, it produces nice tastes too. Cheap.

Leiria

Liz Bar-Restaurant Rua Dr C. Mateus. Serves hearty helpings of fine fare with friendly efficiency. Cheap.

Lisbon

Tagide 18 Largo da Academia Nacional de Belas Artes (tel. 01-320720). Very posh, with reliably delicious dishes and good service. Expensive.

Pap'Acorda 57 Rua da Atalaia (tel. 01-364811). A good choice for Portuguese specialities. Expensive.

Senhor do Vinho 18 Rua do Meio à Lapa (tel. 01-672681). Reputed to be the best *fado* restaurant in town. Expensive.

Comida de Santo 39 Calcada do Eng. Miguel Pais (tel. 01-663339). Brazilian menu and jungle decor. Expensive.

O Tacao Pequeno 3A Travessa da Cara. A cosy and popular dive, full of arty people and knick-knacks. Even the menu is imaginative (try the excellent Algarve squid). Moderate.

O Zé da Conquilha Restaurant-Snack Bar 27 Rua do Rosa. The sort of place you stumble on by serendipity. Regular customers become part of the local 'family', an atmosphere which more than makes up for the limited menu. Cheap.

Miranda do Douro

Restaurant O Mirandês Largo da Moagem (tel. 073-42418). Just outside the city walls, has more charm than most in town, with wood beams and local sketches on the walls. The grilled veal and orange tart are memorably good. Moderate.

Óbidos

Alcaide Rua Direita (tel. 062-95220). A tourist favourite, specializing in dishes from the Azores. The pumpkin and almond cakes are very 'Moorish'. Try and get one of the three balcony tables for evening church bells, bats and setting sun. Moderate.

Olhão

Algarve Restaurant off Rua Marques de Pombal (tel. 089-72470). Serves fine Algarve dishes in a modest setting. Cheap.

Oporto

Portucale 598 Rua da Alegria (tel. 02-570717). Offers excellent views of the city as well as a refined cuisine. Expensive.

Abadia 22 Rua do Ateneu Comercial do Porto (tel. 02-28757). A huge and wonderfully old-fashioned place, popular with local businessmen. Service is very dignified, especially when you order Oporto's famed speciality, *tripas à moda do Oporto*. Moderate.

Casa Peza do Arroz 41 Cais da Ribeira (tel. 02-310291). Like all the restaurants along the Ribeira, very touristy, but if you arrive early it can be a pleasant little nook. Moderate.

A Tasquinha 23 Rua do Carmo. Attracts a clientele of well-dressed couples and prides itself on its folksy decor and extensive wine list. Moderate.

Standard Bar 43 Rua Infante D. Henrique (tel. 02-23904). Provides good food in an attractive, casual setting. Cheap.

Majestic Café 2 Rua Santa Catarina. *The* place for breakfast or snack lunch, with its crumpled leather benches, art deco mirrored walls and suitably Bohemian customers. The other classic in town, **Café Brasileira** (Rua Sa de Bandeira), also serves snacks at the counter.

Ponte de Lima

Gaio Restaurant Rua Agostinho J. Taveira (tel. 058-941251). A cheery place with hearty local fare such as *rôjoes com arroz de sarrabulho,* nuggets of pork with rice mixed with minced meats in pigs' blood (there are alternatives). Cheap.

Sendim

Restaurante Gabriela 28 Largo da Praça (tel. 073-73180). This restaurant has made the undistinguished little town famous: its chef, Alice, won the Golden Cock Award in 1987 for one of the world's best restaurants, and has featured on Portuguese television. Try her winner—*posta Mirandesa à Gabriela*, a thick veal steak in sauce, with salad and chips. Moderate.

Tavira

Patio Restaurant 30 Rua António Cabreira (tel. 081-23008). Geared to tourists, offering tempting specialities (couscous, *cataplana, coq au vin*) on an outdoor patio. Moderate.

O Colmeia 120 Rua do Cais, and nearby **A Barquinha**, are simple fishermen's favourites beside the river. Cheap.

Tomar

Chico Elias Algarvias (tel. 049-311067). Justifiably popular for its fine local fare and relaxed setting. Moderate.

Viana do Castelo

Os 3 Potes 9 Beco dos Fornos (tel. 058-829928). Charms tourists with its folksy hanging hams, black pots and locally embroidered tablecloths (the food's pretty good, too). Saturdays feature Gala Dinners with *fado* and folk dancing. Moderate.

Cozinha das Malheiras 19 Rua Gago Coutinho. Run on more elegant lines, with an enticing menu featuring the likes of langoustine, crabs and lobsters. Moderate. (Across the road is a Casa do Pasto with more modest dishes half the price.)

Viseu

O Cortiço 47 Rua Augusto Hilário (tel. 032-23853). Offers such delicacies as 'rotten cod decayed in the cellar', 'drunken rabbit during three days in life', and 'port fillets by the swineherd,' this cosy bistro is better at its cooking than its English translations. Moderate.

O Hilário 35 Rua Augusto Hilário, named after a famous nineteenth-century *fado* singer born in this street, offers a range of regional specialities. Cheap.

Recommended Reading

History
Livermore, H., *A New History of Portugal* (Cambridge University Press, 1976)
Marques, A.D. de Oliveira, *History of Portugal* (Columbia University Press, 1972)
Nowell, C., *A History of Portugal* (Van Nostrand Co., 1952)
Boxer, C.R., *The Portuguese Seaborne Empire 1415–1825* (Hutchinson, 1977)
Harvey, R., *Portugal: Birth of a Democracy* (Macmillan, 1978)

Literature
Camões, Luís Vaz de, *The Lusiads* (Penguin, 1985)
Queiroz, Eça de, *The Maias* (Dent, 1986); *The Sin of Father Amaro* (Black Swan)
Pessoa, Fernando, *Selected Poems* (Penguin, 1988)
Pires, José Cardoso, *Ballad of Dogs' Beach* (Dent, 1986)
Garrett, Almeida, *Travels in My Homeland* (Peter Owen, 1987)

Travel
Macauley, Rose, *They Went to Portugal* (Penguin, 1985)
Andersen, Hans Christian, *A Visit to Portugal, 1866* (Peter Owen)
Gallop, Rodney, *Portugal, A Book of Folk Ways* (Cambridge University Press, 1969)
Beckford, William, *Recollections of an Excursion to the Monasteries of Alcobaça and Batalha, 1778–88* (Centaur Press, 1972)
Ellingham, Mark, *et al.*, *The Rough Guide to Portugal* (Harrap-Columbus, 1990)
Robertson, I., *Blue Guide: Portugal* (A & C Black, 1988)
Evans, D., *Cadogan Guides: Portugal* (Cadogan Books, 1990)

Food and Drink
Read, J., *The Wines of Portugal* (Faber and Faber, 1987)
Bradford, S., *The Story of Port* (Christie's Wine Publications, 1983)
Vieira, E., *A Taste of Portugal* (Robert Hale, 1988)

Phrase Books
The Portuguese Travelmate (Richard Drew, 1988)
Portuguese at Your Fingertips (Routledge & Kegan Paul, 1986)
Portuguese Phrasebook (Harrap)

Index

ESGB/01/01